HUSH LITTLE BABY

AVERY PUBLISHING GROUP

Garden City Park • New York

Cover designer: Doug Brooks
Typesetter: Richard Morrock
In-House Editor: Elaine Will Sparber

Avery Publishing Group
120 Old Broadway
Garden City Park, NY 11040
1–800–548–5757
www.averypublishing.com

DISCARD

Cataloging-in-Publication Data
Hill, Barbara Albers.
    Hush little baby : gentle methods to stop your baby from crying
/ Barbara Albers Hill.
    p. cm.
    Includes bibliographical references and index.
    ISBN 0-89529-994-1
    1. Crying in infants Popular works. 2. Infants (Newborn)—Care
Popular works. 3. Infants—Care Popular works. 4. Child rearing
Popular works. I. Title.
    RJ61.H555 1999
    649'.122—dc21
                                            99-39166
                                            CIP

Copyright © 1999 by Barbara Albers Hill

Printed in the United States of America

10 9 8 7 6 5 4 3 2 1

Contents

Preface

Not too long ago, my family journeyed to a local beach, setting our blanket and chairs amid a sea of other parents and children. At one point, three infants in our vicinity began to wail almost simultaneously, and I was struck by their parents' similar reactions. As one, the parents bent down, scooped up their criers, and began to sway from side to side while whispering soothing words. Two of the babies quieted down at once; the third seemed oblivious to his father's calming presence, howling even louder as Dad's swaying grew more vigorous.

These babies' different responses brought back memories of my own baby-calming efforts, reminding me of that first jarring realization that rocking my crying baby didn't quiet him all the time. For that matter, neither did feeding him, singing to him, tempting him with a toy, taking him out of doors, or any of the other myriad distractions I could think of. True, these tactics all had occasional success as calming mechanisms, but I learned early on that the tinkling mobile that turned baby sobs to smiles at eight o'clock in the morning might well have been playing in my neighbor's house at nightfall, for all the impact it had on post-dinner fussiness. Those evening wails stemmed from a vastly different source than the tears my baby shed at other times of day.

Though I knew that my baby's crying could signal anything from fright to boredom to plain old hunger, it was a while before I could pinpoint what each of the specific or regularly recurring cries meant. It was longer still before I understood that I needed to match my response to the cause of my baby's misery. Through time-consuming trial and error, I eventually learned what worked and what didn't to soothe him.

I hope that sharing my discoveries, as well as those of other veteran parents, in *Hush Little Baby* will minimize the uncertainty that you may feel while trying to calm your crying baby. Enjoy browsing through the ideas and suggestions that follow. And, may your introduction to parenthood be made more enjoyable as a result of your reading.

A Word
About Gender

Your baby is certainly as likely to be a boy as a girl. However, the English language does not provide a genderless pronoun. Therefore, to avoid the use of the awkward "he/she" when referring to a child and still give equal time to both sexes, the masculine pronouns "he," "him," and "his" are used in the odd-numbered chapters, and the female pronouns "she," "her," and "hers" are used in the rest. This has been done in the interest of simplicity and clarity.

Introduction

"This morning, Shannon relaxed at once when I bounced her on my knee to calm her crying. Tonight, I tried the same thing, and she cried so hard that she threw up. Will 'horsy ride' restore her good mood the next time she cries? I'm not sure I want to find out!"

—Mary P., mother of four-month-old Shannon

If you have ever had success with a baby-soothing method only to try it later and find that it is making matters worse, you can probably sympathize with Shannon's mother. And you're in good company! It's hardly a secret that babies cry a lot—a total of six, twelve, or even eighteen hours a day. And babies who cry twenty different times during the day may be voicing twenty separate complaints. Why so much misery? Because babies' needs are all-encompassing, and babies lack another means of communication. They cry when they are hungry, of course, but they also wail when they are stressed, ill, cold, tired, gassy, restless, frustrated, fearful . . . the list goes on and on.

As babies get older, it becomes easier to decode their various cries, but at any age, what soothes their misery must touch at its cause. Rocking, for instance, will calm a colicky baby, but make an overstimulated tyke even more frantic. A darkened room won't soothe an infant who feels ill, but will work wonders to quiet one who cries each day at sunrise. And, a ride in a front-pack carrier will distract a teething baby, but further frighten an anxious one.

1

Does this sort of match-up game sound like an experimentation process designed to wreak havoc with your busy life? *Hush Little Baby* can hasten your success. Each chapter covers a different cause of baby distress, with tips specially tailored to the crying that results. You'll find practical information, strategies for identifying your baby's cries, anecdotes from real parents, and dozens of useful tips for getting at—and erasing—the cause of your baby's fussiness.

If your infant is among the 40 percent who are affected by colic, Chapter 1 will give you insights and answers. Crying due to overstimulation, that upsetting sense of bombardment, is addressed in Chapter 2. Feeding-related crying, whether the result of hunger, gas, or overzealous sucking, is examined in detail in Chapter 3. Chapter 4, covering crying due to physical discomfort, will help you pinpoint problems and ensure your baby's state of well-being. More urgent medical situations and the crying that accompanies them are discussed in Chapter 5.

The experience of frustration builds character, but reduces many babies to tears in the process. Chapter 6 will help you identify and address the circumstances that trigger a baby's angry wails. In Chapter 7, you'll find information on and help for crying that is stress- or anxiety-related, while attention-seeking crying and a baby's need for entertainment are examined in Chapter 8. The final chapter, Chapter 9, is devoted to the effects of a baby's frequent crying on the rest of the family. As in the other chapters, you'll find background material and specific suggestions to help you cope with this most demanding aspect of infancy.

Crying is an expected component of babyhood. Your little one's wails and whimpers are her way of summoning you, requesting assistance, and, ultimately, revealing her sociability level and array of likes and dislikes. To be sure, you won't always be certain why your baby is crying, nor will you always have a magical antidote at hand. But reading and shopping among the tactics that follow will give you an increased awareness of your baby's ever-changing moods and help you become more attuned to her personal sensitivities. By matching your calming technique to the source of her distress, you'll find that you can restore her smile—and your own—with speed and efficiency. Best of luck!

1

Colicky Crying

For four weeks, dinnertime at the Wilton household was a nightmare. At around five o'clock each day, the family's seven-week-old baby began to fuss and squirm, within minutes working himself into a red-faced frenzy that lasted until eleven o'clock or later. The Wiltons tried valiantly to head off their baby's daily bout with colic, but nothing calmed him for more than a few minutes. One night, a desperate Dan Wilton threw a blanket around his squalling infant and, clutching the boy tightly, strode around the neighborhood. Oblivious to the threat of rain and the mosquitoes feasting on his neck and arms, Dan kept walking with his now-quiet son. After the month his family had just endured, no price was too great for an evening of peace.

The crying that is associated with infant colic has been the subject of study for decades. Theories abound about the causes of and best remedies for colic, but the fact remains that hours of inconsolable screaming on a daily basis take a toll on your baby, your nerves, and your confidence in your ability as a parent. Chapter 1 explores the most commonly accepted explanations for infant colic and helps you determine whether your baby's daily crying spells are a function of this malady. In addition, the chapter presents techniques for minimizing a colicky infant's discomfort—and, ultimately, his howls of misery. If your baby is among the many newborns who suffer from colic, you'll find help and reassurance in the pages that follow.

A TEST

Are the following statements true or false?

1. A newborn's temperament during the first two weeks of life is not a measure of whether he'll be troubled by colic.

2. Colic affects a large percentage of infants.

3. Colicky crying can last through the first year of life.

All of the above statements are true. Researchers say that colic affects more than 700,000 infants, or nearly 40 percent of the babies born each year, causing crying spells that last from three hours to almost around the clock. Colic tends to surface without warning during the second or third week of life, and, while the related crying often improves by the twelfth week, it can easily last six, eight, or even ten months. "Colic," a word derived from the Greek *kolikos*—having to do with the large intestine—has been the target of study for nearly sixty years, but the topic still creates much dissent among infant specialists.

WHAT YOU SHOULD KNOW

Doctors have long since lain to rest the notion that colic stems from the way parents handle their baby. Whether you're relaxed or tense, supremely confident or quite uncertain of your parenting skills, your baby is equally likely to be affected by colic. In recent years, maternal high blood pressure during pregnancy has been suggested as a contributing factor, as have premature or difficult birth, long-lasting labor, and the use of epidural anesthesia. While studies have linked each of these conditions with more intense, less adaptable infants, it's important to realize that competing research has found no such correlations.

At present, digestive immaturity is under close scrutiny as the cause of colic. Lactose and certain starches create excess acid and gas in the lower intestinal tract, with cramping often the result. In addition, the infant stomach has few gastric glands, and the intestines have little surface texture to assist in the processing of milk or formula. Food moves spasmodically through the digestive tract, but the rhythmic motion of peristalsis is absent during the early weeks of life. All in all, digestion has the potential to cause an infant significant discomfort.

Nevertheless, a number of specialists insist that, despite the pained appearance of the screaming colicky baby, there is no physiological cause for his distress. Instead, they suggest that the malady is psychosomatic—an end-of-day fussy period that stresses tired parents, who transmit their impatience and rising tension to their equally worn-out baby. The baby, in turn, gulps excess air into an intestinal tract already overstimulated by his screaming, resulting in painful pockets of gas and even more agonized wails.

WHAT YOU'LL EXPERIENCE

How can you be certain that your baby's prolonged crying episodes are, in fact, caused by colic? Most infant specialists agree that true colic leaves no room for doubt. The related cries are markedly different from babies' other cries and diminish only momentarily, if at all, in the face of the usual comforting methods.

While an infant's cries of hunger or boredom begin as fussing and escalate only in the absence of a response, crying from colic occurs without warning. A colicky baby stiffens his limbs or jerks as if struck by a sudden jolt, then gives out an intense, high-pitched wail that seems to signal pain. His face reddens with the force of his screams, his abdomen seems rigid, and he draws his arms and legs up tight against his body, toes and fists clenched. When you check the baby for a physical cause to his misery, you find his diaper dry, and his clothing and blanket intact and free of sharp or protruding objects. When you cuddle him, rock him, place him on his stomach, or change his surroundings, your efforts provide only momentary distraction, after which his frantic screams begin anew. Even a feeding doesn't help, for a full stomach lacks its usual calming effect and your baby resumes his screeching almost as soon as he finishes sucking.

Unlike everyday fussing, episodes of colicky crying can be as long-lasting as they are resistant to your efforts to end them. Each time, after an hour or so of fruitless cradling and rocking, you anticipate your shrieking baby's collapse into an exhausted, but blessedly quiet sleep. Instead, his howling persists for two or three hours more—or spans ten, fifteen, or twenty hours, with a few fretful catnaps providing your only respite from the harsh sounds of his cries. Many times, a pattern will emerge, with the wailing beginning between six o'clock and nine o'clock in the evening. The reason for this is unclear, with morning-to-night fluctuations in your breast milk or the baby's cortisone, prostaglandin, or progesterone level under consideration as causes. It has also been suggested that late-day fatigue compromises a baby's ability to filter out unwanted stimulation.

During the weeks your baby struggles with colic, you will likely find yourself searching endlessly for the conditions that trigger his daily bouts of screaming, despite assurances from your family, friends, and baby's doctor that time is the only real antidote. You may vary your daily routine and make changes in your baby's surroundings in the hope that you'll stumble upon the secret to a peaceful night. You may work just as hard to find ways to lessen the intensity and duration of his crying. Unfortunately, you may make matters worse by trying and rejecting a great many calming tactics, thereby overwhelming your baby with a barrage of sights and sensations in a short period of time. When your valiant efforts fail to meet with long-term success, you may become greatly discouraged, as well as drained, helpless, weepy, and embarrassed by your baby's impossible behavior.

WHAT YOU CAN DO

Happily, you can do more than just sit by and wait for your baby to outgrow his colic. While baby-calming techniques come without guarantees, and while a tactic that soothes your baby today may fail to work tomorrow, you'll feel better about your baby's daily descent into hysteria if you take steps to help him relax.

Often, the secret to soothing a colicky baby lies in introducing a stimulus that is distracting and pleasing enough to hold his attention for up to a minute. The longer you can silence your baby's cries, the calmer he will become. Ultimately, your goal is to ease him into sleep. Because too much variety may confuse and overwhelm your baby, you should not try the technique that worked the first time if he awakens still in misery. When one calming method begins to lose its charm, whether after one day or several, you should move on to other strategies. You may wish to consider the suggestions that follow, which have worked to quiet the howls of other colicky babies.

Anticipate Your Baby's Screaming Episodes

Once colic surfaces, your baby will almost certainly be affected at the same time each day. Plan ahead, accomplishing what you can early in the day, to ensure that you are ready to give your full attention to comforting your baby when he needs it.

Recreate Your Baby's Former Environment

Simulate your baby's life in the womb by putting him to sleep in pitch darkness. Even a blackout shade lets in light around the edges, so add an additional window covering of opaque fabric. Put your baby down wearing a hat, with the top of his head nestled against the crib or cradle bumper, and add a ticking clock to mimic a heartbeat.

Keep Your Baby Far From the Kitchen at Dinnertime

Cooking smells so often seem to trigger episodes of colic—even among just-fed, sleeping infants—that some researchers have begun to wonder if food aromas trigger a reaction in the infant's digestive system. Try altering your mealtime, as well as cooking in bulk and reheating in the microwave. In addition, try putting your baby to sleep behind a closed door before you uncover and serve your meal.

Massage Your Baby

You can minimize any gastrointestinal discomfort your baby may be feeling by firmly massaging his stomach and abdomen. Place one of your hands below the left side of his rib cage and move it in a clockwise direction, down and across his lower torso, then up to the base of the right side of his rib cage. This motion may calm him, since it helps move trapped gas through the intestinal tract.

Swaddle Your Baby

Many uncomfortable or distressed infants find confinement to be soothing. Try wrapping your baby tightly in a receiving blanket or tucking him into a sling or front-pack carrier. You can also try lying on your back, knees bent, and holding your baby snugly against your chest with both arms.

Provide Continuous, Monotonous Sound

Many parents have discovered the soothing power of "white noise," such as the hum of a vacuum cleaner, dehumidifier, or fan, or the sound of a running shower. The louder the drone is, the better it will snatch your baby's attention away from both-

Why Not Try Whiskey?

Rubbing liquor on a baby's sore gums, or mixing it into his water or formula, was for generations recommended as a solution to colicky crying. Today, most parents know better than to give babies alcohol of any sort. Just a drop or two has been known to cause infants sleeplessness and such dangerous physical conditions as tremors, changes in the blood-sugar level, and severe sweating.

Alcohol has a depressant effect on adults, but it affects babies far differently. Whatever well-meaning relatives and friends may advise, you should never be tempted to quiet your baby with liquor.

ersome stimuli. A recording of your baby's favorite sound will probably work just as well as the actual noise.

Use Home Remedies

Many parents have successfully cut down their babies' colicky crying by giving them two to three teaspoons of fennel, bay leaf, or chamomile tea, served plain or mixed with breast milk or formula. Other parents have headed off crying spells by feeding their babies a few teaspoons of ginger ale, warm water, or plain yogurt, all of which lessen intestinal gas. You can also place a partly filled, towel-wrapped hot water bottle against your baby's abdomen to further reduce his discomfort.

Consider Pharmaceutical Products

An infant-sized glycerin suppository will help your crying baby pass painful gas. Simethicone drops, squirted directly into his mouth following feedings, can reduce gas buildup during digestion. Prescription antispasmodics, which ease intestinal cramping, are another option you may wish to explore. Of course, you should talk with your baby's doctor before trying medical remedies of any type.

Reposition Your Baby

Keep your infant in a near-sitting position during feedings so that less air passes from his stomach to his intestines. Experiment with different holds that place gentle pressure on his abdomen, such as facedown along your forearm with his pelvis supported by your upturned hand or facedown across your knees. Try propping your baby on his side at naptime and placing him stomach-down on a warmed blanket or pad during awake periods.

Distract Your Baby With Movement

A gentle back-and-forth or shaking motion may appeal to your baby's tactile sense and successfully soothe his wails. A closely

---

It's Not Your Fault!

Over the years, it has often been suggested that maternal tension is largely responsible for a baby's experience with colic. Many have said that babies sense and are so distressed by their mothers' anxiety that they react with inconsolable crying. If this is the case, why do many couples experience colic with one child, but not with another? Why do some calm parents have high-need babies, while some intense parents have offspring that are quite mellow?

It is true that studies have shown a greater frequency of colicky babies among mothers who score high on the anxiety segment of various personality tests. However, this stress may well be the result, not the cause, of their babies' hours of crying. And, mothers who report feeling anxious before their baby's birth may simply be less objective at labeling their infant's behavior—and less adept at soothing his wails of anguish—than they are likely to have colicky babies in the first place.

Ultimately, you shouldn't worry that your baby's colicky crying spells are your fault. It's more productive to focus on soothing your little one's misery than to spend time feeling responsible for his discomfort.

---

supervised ride atop a running clothes dryer or in a battery-operated swing that continues without interruption may work as well, as may a ride in the car. You may also be able to quiet your baby with a device called Sleep-Tight (available by calling 1–800–662–6542), which can be attached to the springs of his

Misconceptions About Colic

Despite having been thoroughly studied, infant colic is still very much misunderstood. Following are five of the most common myths concerning colic:

1. *Infant colic is an illness.* Though your colicky baby may seem gassy during his extended bouts of screaming, his discomfort is not thought to be the cause of his distress, but the result of his gulping of air.

2. *Colicky crying is manipulative behavior.* Whether your baby screams for an hour or an entire evening, he is conveying true distress and will be comforted—not spoiled—by your response.

3. *Colic is related to bottle-feeding.* The malady occurs with equal frequency among all infants, whether breast- or bottle-fed.

4. *Colic is a function of birth order and gender.* Research does not support the long-held notion that colic occurs most frequently among firstborn males.

5. *Colic appears with greater frequency among premature and highly sensitive babies.* Many babies who are born early or who react strongly to light, sound, or motion remain wholly unaffected by colic.

Pondering the particulars of colic may give you a small sense of control over your baby's prolonged crying, but giving your baby loving attention is the surest way to soothe his distress.

crib and simulates the motion of a car traveling at fifty-five miles per hour.

Try Music

If you play a pleasing song as soon as your baby begins fussing, he may stop crying to listen. As he loses interest in the song, play a different one. Eventually, you may be able to use music to calm your baby whenever he is fussy, but be sure to turn it off whenever he wails in earnest. If he enjoys listening, he'll soon realize that crying causes his music to disappear.

Positive Reinforcement

Pay attention to your baby when he is calm and quiet. If you tend to leave his side for long periods when he is contented, he will quickly associate quiet behavior with solitude and crying with gaining your focus. In particular, talk to him, and make plenty of eye contact during his most alert, receptive times.

For many infants, the experience of colic is inevitable. If your baby is among the many destined to wrestle with this puzzling syndrome, you can minimize his distress as well as yours by helping him through each episode with tactics designed to make him feel safe, comfortable, and loved.

In the years to come, researchers may conclude that infant colic stems from digestive deficiency, or sensory immaturity, or perhaps some kind of genetic predisposition. Many infant specialists are already certain that science will find several contributing factors, rather than a single reason, for the seeming agony endured by infants with colic.

Whatever the force and duration of your colicky baby's crying episodes, you can take heart in the knowledge that he will bear no ill effects from his weeks or months of misery. In addition, no matter what his personal timetable, his colic will fade almost as quickly as it began. He will, indeed, pass through this very difficult stage, emerging as a personable, predictable baby who is delightfully easy to care for. And in the long run, you may even conclude that the extra care you lavished on your baby during his colicky stage has helped him become a more secure, confident child.

2

Crying Due to Overstimulation

Jill Holden's baby is surprisingly alert for just two months old. The infant's wide-open eyes are constantly on the move in search of new people to study and new sights to behold. Recognizing their baby's fascination with her surroundings, the Holdens frequently take their child on outings. Unfortunately, these well-meant sojourns often end on a sour note, with screeching infant and puzzled parents having to leave abruptly for home.

Jill and her husband can't understand why the visual stimulation that delights their baby one minute can suddenly send her into a crying frenzy the next. After all, aren't looking and watching the activities the infant most enjoys? The Holdens have pondered their destinations, the baby's schedule, and even their physical handling of the child as possible reasons for her public meltdowns, but cannot determine the cause of the distress. Last week, after a particularly trying visit to a relative's block party, Jill threatened to keep the infant closeted at home. "If I get any more of these mixed signals," she warned, only half joking, "this baby is going to become a recluse!"

Does your infant ever fall apart without warning amid fascinating sights, sounds, or activities? If so, you can probably sympathize with the Holdens' dilemma. Their baby's response exemplifies stimulus overload, a condition that occurs when a baby tries—and fails—to absorb an overabundance of sensory information. Chapter 2 gives the facts about this phenomenon and describes how to assess a baby's sensory-input threshold. The chapter also presents strategies for providing babies with the right amount of stimulation. A great many infants decompress when they spend time in busy surroundings. What you'll read in this chapter can help you handle this tricky stage—without taking your baby into hiding.

DO YOU RECOGNIZE THIS CHILD?

"My baby finds music tremendously entertaining. She also has a lot of trouble settling down for naps, so I thought that leaving a radio playing would help her to fall asleep. Instead, she listens quietly for a few seconds and then starts to cry and twist around in her crib as if trying to get away from the sound. If she loves music so much, why doesn't my strategy work to relax her?"

The baby just described seems to have a strong auditory sense. It's quite likely that she enjoys listening to conversation, television noise, and the sounds of nature as much as she does her beloved music. Because this baby cannot escape her environment, however, she continues to absorb sensory input even when she is too tired to process the information. The result is overstimulation, a sense of bombardment that a baby may find uncomfortable, unpleasant, and, as her parents quickly learn, quite objectionable.

WHAT YOU SHOULD KNOW

Even in infancy, babies vary greatly in their sensitivity to their surroundings. The more extreme their attunement is to the sensory input they favor, the more riveted they will be by even fleeting colors and shapes, sounds, or movements. A visually sensitive baby may not sleep if there is light in the room, while an auditorally attuned infant may not feed well if there are people talking nearby. The baby who is sensitive to touch and motion is acutely aware of her own body, startling at her own movements and resisting attempts to rock her to sleep. Given the amount and variety of stimulation offered by the average household, a baby's end-of-day sensory overload is easily understandable.

A newborn baby is at first protected against overstimulation by her immature nervous system. In the early days, she is able to process only a few incoming stimuli at a time—specifically, the strongest signals, such as hunger pangs or loud noise. Lesser sensory input, such as television noise, a bobbing crib mobile, or the sensation of rocking, is overlooked. After two weeks, however, the baby begins to pick up on much more of the input from her environment, finding it fascinating, but quickly overwhelming. A young baby gives almost no warning that she is going into sensory overload, but parents who recognize and stay alert to the initial signals of meltdown can move their little one to a more peaceful surrounding.

The baby who is weary of watching, listening, or otherwise sensing her environment may try squeezing her eyes shut or turning away from the source of her stimulation. Some babies appear to suddenly fall asleep amid the commotion, though doing so is more a shutting down of the senses than a means of getting rest. Interestingly, this shutdown ability vanishes during the second month of life, leaving a stimulus-control gap that lasts until toddlerhood, when babies can physically move to different surroundings when they feel overloaded. (The ability to mentally filter out unwanted sensory input doesn't develop until the preschool years.) When shying away from environmental stimuli fails to bring the peace and quiet your baby craves, you can count on her to convey her distress the only way she can—by crying.

WHAT YOU'LL EXPERIENCE

Fussiness from overstimulation is primarily a late-afternoon problem. However, if your baby is unusually sensitive or has had a hectic day, it may occur earlier. Tired despite her usual series of naps, your baby will start to feel annoyed by incoming stimuli, and squirm and complain in a fruitless attempt to make the sights, sounds, or tactile input go away. At first, you may mistake her restlessness for boredom and step up your entertainment efforts, but you will quickly find that distraction techniques do not work and, in fact, increase your baby's irritability.

As she fusses, your overloaded baby will close her eyes or turn her head away from you, but the tenseness of her body will tell you that she isn't really asleep. She may want to suck continuously, not because she is hungry, but as a soothing mechanism. However, since she cannot relax, any nourishment she takes won't have its usual calming effect. As your baby's distress increases, she may pull her knees and arms up close to her body, a position that usually helps her feel more secure and in control of her environment.

You may be surprised at how quickly your baby moves into complete sensory overload. Depending on her level of awareness of environmental stimuli, her degree of fatigue, and the type of day she has had, the time between initial late-day fussiness and a state of hysteria can be as little as five minutes. To avoid complete meltdown, it is important to learn and respond to your baby's earliest signals of overstimulation.

WHAT YOU CAN DO

You can do a lot to avoid overstimulating your baby by remembering how much in her environment is brand new to her. Even at home, where the sights and sounds are quite familiar, circumstances such as unexpected company or your own brisker-than-normal work pace can keep your baby in a state of attention. To minimize sensory overload, or to calm your baby when she's in the throes of hysteria, you may wish to try one of the following techniques.

Help Your Baby to Experience Quiet

For now, keep your baby's playtimes short and relaxed, and keep her daytime surroundings subdued and softly lit. At night, make her sleeping area as dark and silent as possible.

Pay Attention to Your Baby's Body Language

Become aware of the warning signs your baby generally displays when she is feeling frazzled by too much commotion. You may find eye-rubbing, head-turning, or sudden naps to be cues that she needs some peace and quiet.

Make Naps a Priority

For now, adjust the family's schedule so that your baby can sleep when, and for as long as, she needs to. You'll find that your little one can cope with her surroundings better—and longer—when she is well rested.

Take a Stroll Together

Tuck your overstimulated baby into a front-pack carrier and go for a long walk. She will relax for as long as you keep moving.

When a Baby "Tunes Out"

A baby who shuts down by closing her eyes to excessive or unpleasant stimuli may appear peaceful-looking and at ease. However, even though "playing possum" is less stressful than processing noise or commotion, it is not relaxing. Nor does it yield quality sleep.

How can you tell whether your baby is catnapping or simply retreating from excess sights and sounds? The answer lies in her mood upon reopening her eyes. If she seems content, she is probably feeling refreshed. If she is cranky, however, you'll know she wasn't resting and needs your help to create a quieter environment.

Establish Your Baby's Crib, Cradle, or Bassinet as a Restful Place

Resist the urge to use your baby's sleep space as a daytime play area, and keep it free of stuffed animals, mobiles, and other visual distractions.

Settle Your Baby to Sleep in a Fairly Small Space

Using a bassinet or cradle, or lining a crib with cloth bumpers against which your baby can nestle her head may have a calming effect. Many babies are reassured by the sense of confinement.

Help Your Baby Learn to Relax Herself

Provide your little one with a pacifier, or keep her hands exposed for sucking. Put her down for naps when she is calm, well fed, and almost, but not quite, asleep.

Calm Your Overwrought Baby With "White Noise"

The drone of a fan, clothes dryer, or vacuum cleaner, or a tape recording of such machine noise, can keep your little one from tuning in to conversation and household sounds.

The Importance of Stepping In

"If your infant seems extraordinarily alert or subsists on brief catnaps all day long, she'll probably have trouble winding down in the evening. And until she works out her own calming method, wailing may be the only way she can decompress.

"Will your crying infant become spoiled by your holding or rocking her? Absolutely not! As hard as it may seem to believe when your baby is shrieking inconsolably into your ear, your comforting presence provides her with a wonderful sense of security."

—Adapted from *Baby Tactics: Parenting Tips That Really Work* by Barbara Albers Hill

Try a Calming Focal Point

Consider using a lighted aquarium or lava lamp in an otherwise darkened room to help soothe your overstimulated baby.

Provide a Physical Sense of Security

Try swaddling your fussy baby in a receiving blanket. Preventing her limbs from flailing will reduce tactile stimulation and help her to relax.

Swing or Rock Your Crying Baby

Relentless motion, particularly in a darkened, silent room, can help your overwrought baby block out irritating sights and sounds.

Shield Your Infant From Excessive Sights

When you are away from home, consider limiting your baby's visual stimulation by draping a towel over the car window next to her infant seat or tossing a blanket over the stroller as you go walking. (Naturally, you'll want to check on your baby frequently.)

Using the Right Moves

When soothing an overwrought baby, the success of your calming technique will depend on the innate appeal of the particular response it causes in her. "Tactics that relax one baby may heap additional stimulation on the next," says Dr. Lauren Bradway, coauthor of *How to Maximize Your Child's Learning Ability* (Garden City Park, NY: Avery Publishing Group, 1993). "The answer lies in your baby's inborn sensory style." A stroll out of doors, for instance, provides much to look at and so may not do much to calm a highly visual baby. One who is more attuned to sound, however, may love it. Similarly, bouncing or rocking is likely to be least soothing to babies who thrive on motion and touch.

"When your baby seems overloaded, it's a good idea to remove her from the kinds of stimuli she loves best," says Dr. Bradway. "She'll be more able to relax when her preferred sense is given some time off."

Offer the Reassurance of Full-Body Contact

Help a truly frantic baby to shut out stimulation by lying on your back and hugging her, chest-to-chest, in a pitch-dark, silent room.

On a positive note, the routine changes you enact to tone down your baby's surroundings need only be temporary. As your little one grows, her tolerance for visual, auditory, and tactile input will more closely mirror her enjoyment of it. Stay close to home if you must during your baby's overly sensitive phase, and experiment with one or more of the aforementioned comforting tactics during times of overload. By doing what you can to keep stimulation at a tolerable level, you'll help both your baby and yourself to be calmer and happier.

Crying Related
to Feeding

L ena's four-week-old son is a voracious eater, shrieking
for food before his eyes are fully opened and draining
eight-ounce bottles in minutes. The baby howls in outrage when a feeding is halted midway through for burping
purposes, so Lena and her husband usually let him finish his
bottles uninterrupted. Unfortunately, the infant's frantic gulping causes him to swallow a good deal of air along with the formula. This, in turn, causes him to tense up, cry, and, all too
often, spit up the entire feeding as soon as the adult in charge
turns him upright. At this point, his stomach as empty as
before, he begins screaming anew.

When this happens, Lena is uncertain whether to re-feed
her ravenous baby immediately or hold him off while his
stomach settles a bit. She has tried both strategies with little
success—a second bottle usually comes back up as quickly as
the first, while attempts to buy a little time result in the baby
being too overwrought or too tired to suck until he is full.

Does your baby cry more than you'd like around feeding
time? If so, you'll find Chapter 3 most helpful. You'll find out

why infant feedings can have a less-than-soothing effect and get help determining what may be causing your baby's discomfort. You'll also read about downplaying night feedings, introducing solid food, and minimizing food-related crying of all types. Each baby's sucking habits are unique, and trial and error is often the best antidote to feeding-related fussiness. This chapter will guide you as you negotiate your baby's particular wants and needs.

DO YOU RECOGNIZE THIS CHILD?

"Our baby cries for a feeding once an hour 'round the clock."

"My infant gets so worked up when he's hungry that there's no rhythm to his sucking and gulping."

"My baby is so relaxed by feeding that he falls asleep after just a few swallows."

It is well established in the child-rearing literature that feeding time meets much more than a baby's nutritional needs. Holding your baby while you breast- or bottle-feed lets you cuddle, comfort, and communicate with him. Why, then, do some parents have trouble feeding their babies? It may surprise you to learn that a crying baby isn't always soothed by the breast or bottle—in fact, his eating habits and your feeding techniques can sometimes compound his discomfort and distress. When this happens, additional nourishment—however well meant—may cause your little one's cries to escalate rather than diminish.

WHAT YOU SHOULD KNOW

Feeding your baby is as much about social interaction as about nourishment. While it may take your infant weeks to establish a feeding pattern, he will realize pretty quickly that loving arms are involved. And, for you, feeding is the baby-care task that most often includes time to relax and enjoy your little one. Therefore, you'll surely want to uncover the source of any agitation your baby experiences while feeding. To that end, there are a number of things to consider.

A crying baby is clearly uncomfortable. According to infant specialists, however, thirst can be ruled out as the problem. Both breast milk and formula contain all the water a baby needs. Though your cranky baby may accept a water bottle if it's offered, hunger—not thirst—compels him to suck.

If your baby seems to experience stomach discomfort at feeding time, food sensitivity or a digestive problem may be at work. Or, your baby may be swallowing more air with his milk than your current burping technique can expel. Applying pressure to your baby's abdomen with one hand while firmly rubbing the middle of his back with your other hand should do the trick, especially after a big feeding. However, you may need to experiment to find the most efficient burping position.

Restlessness and intermittent fussing can signal that your little one feels lonely. This problem will correct itself as soon as you learn how—and how much—he likes to socialize during feedings. Until then, it's a good idea to talk softly or keep up eye contact while he eats.

WHAT YOU'LL EXPERIENCE

Feeding-related distress can take a number of different forms. Early in the feeding, your baby may suddenly stop sucking and turn his head away, almost as if he is trying to get away from you and the nourishment you are offering. Hungry as he seems, your little one may arch his back and purse his lips as you present the breast or bottle, to avoid taking the nipple. Or, he may simply stop swallowing, crying while milk trickles out of his open mouth.

Your baby's misery may even begin while he is sucking. You may note that he squirms uncomfortably or pulls in his legs as if tensing against increasing abdominal discomfort. Or, he may be jolted from his relaxed state, crying as if struck. Another possibility is that he drifts off to sleep at the breast or bottle, but is startled when he is burped or put down, and thus screams.

Crying of this nature can certainly be your baby's way of communicating hunger, but feeding-related complaints can also indicate physical discomfort, overfeeding, exhaustion, or overstimulation. It is important, but often takes time, to learn to read your baby's signals. With practice, you'll be able to meet your little one's feeding needs with the certainty that your tactics are on target.

WHAT YOU CAN DO

If you find that your crying baby exhibits distress instead of the calm, efficient sucking you expect during a feeding, it may be necessary to alter part of your approach to his mealtime. Following are some techniques to consider.

Avoid Strenuous Exercise During the Hour Before Breast-Feeding

Physical exertion causes the release of a substance that can alter the taste of your milk. Your baby may respond better if you exercise after, not before, his feeding.

Wake Your Baby for a Late-Evening Feeding

Infants rarely sleep for seven-hour stretches. As a result, they can be dismayingly alert at 2:00 A.M. You may be able to cir-

Do Not Disturb!

Because your young baby lacks a sense of day versus night, he may feel so playful in the wee hours that he'll howl when you return him to his bed after a nighttime feeding. Hard as it may be to resist your little one's bids for your attention, you'll help him return to sleep by minimizing interaction at this time. Here's what to do:

- *Feed your baby in his room.* When the house is still, your baby may be more aware of changes in room temperature or street noise. Staying put avoids these stimuli.

- *Keep the room lights low.* Feeding your baby in semi-darkness will minimize visual distractions and eye contact, and the wakefulness that may result.

- *Change your baby's diaper before feeding him.* Your baby's post-feeding drowsiness will encourage him to quickly return to sleep.

- *Place a heating pad on your baby's bed while he is feeding.* Warmed sheets will help prevent your just-fed baby from being jarred from his relaxed, satisfied state.

- *Feed your baby in silence.* Your little one is so attuned to your voice that even whispers or hums can increase his wakefulness.

The more socially rewarding your baby's early-morning feedings are, the more he'll protest when you try to break away. Ultimately, disturbing him as little as possible at night will be less upsetting for you both.

cumvent nighttime problems by putting your baby down with a full stomach at 11:30 P.M. or so. Or, try maximizing your own resources by going to bed for the night when your baby does.

31

What About Solids?

As recently as a generation ago, it was felt that cereal would keep a baby's hunger pangs at bay longer than breast milk or formula. Babies as young as two weeks old had rice cereal mixed into their bottles, particularly at bedtime.

Doctors and baby-care experts now know that young babies lack the muscle control necessary for successful spoon-feeding. In addition, adding cereal to a bottle is frowned upon because infants are more likely to manifest food allergies and digestive difficulties in the early months than after six months of age.

When your baby's caloric needs outpace his liquid diet, usually at between six and nine months of age, his doctor will recommend the introduction of solid food. Here are some suggestions to help make the transition smooth:

• Avoid mixing solids into bottles of breast milk or formula, as this can mean a too-sudden increase in food intake.

Allow Prolonged Sucking After Feeding

Some babies remain awake while they take their nourishment, then continue to suck gently as they drift off to sleep. Keep your baby at your breast or the bottle for a few extra minutes, or offer him a pacifier.

- Use a tiny, pointed spoon at first to allow your baby to suck at the cereal.

- Prop your baby upright to ensure that his swallowing is effective.

- Take the edge off your baby's hunger by nursing or bottle-feeding him for a few minutes before beginning to spoon-feed him. Offer him the rest of his milk afterward.

- Introduce your baby to solids with rice cereal, the least allergenic type of cereal.

- After introducing rice cereal into your baby's diet, wait a week and add a teaspoon of puréed fruit.

- Introduce new foods at one-week intervals so that you can determine which foods, if any, cause digestive discomfort.

The introduction of solid food is a milestone. However, your baby's immature digestive system may experience a few ups and downs during the transition period. With practice and patience, your baby will soon view mealtime as one of the highlights of his day.

Experiment With Hypoallergenic Formulas

Your baby may do better with a soy-based formula than a milk-based one. Soy-based formulas are somewhat less allergenic than those that are milk-based. Or, your baby may better tolerate formula with hydrolyzed (partially digested) protein.

Digestive Difficulties

Sometimes, a baby will take a feeding without fuss or commotion, but will exhibit discomfort shortly afterward. If your little one is an efficient breast- or bottle-feeder, but seems miserable after eating, you may want to speak to his doctor about the following difficulties:

Gastroesophageal reflux (GER). Occasionally, a baby partially regurgitates his stomach acids, causing a burning in his esophagus similar to that of adult heartburn. If your baby's post-feeding crying sounds painful, if he frequently seems congested, or if he often spits up after eating, his doctor may recommend:

- Breast-feeding. GER tends to occur less frequently in breast-fed babies.

- Small, frequent feedings. The antacid properties in milk can be soothing.

- "Wearing" your baby when his stomach is full. Some parents report that chest-to-chest contact and gentle movement seem to improve a baby's digestion.

- Turning to cereal. Your baby's doctor may recommend following feedings with a bit of rice cereal to thicken the contents of the baby's stomach.

Gas. Immature digestive systems make abdominal gas a certainty for almost every infant. However, only some babies become truly uncomfortable. If your baby's abdomen often rumbles or seems distended, or if he frequently pulls up his legs as if trying to pass gas, you may wish to try these tactics:

- Respond quickly to your baby's crying. Air gulped during a crying episode can increase abdominal gas.

- Feed your baby more frequently. Feeding your baby on demand may reduce how much air he gulps.

- Encourage good positioning. Hold your baby at an angle of 45 degrees while he eats and for a half-hour afterward. Also, make sure his lips surround your areola or the base of the bottle nipple.

- Burp your baby two or more times during feedings. Experiment to find the position and frequency that most please your baby.

Food sensitivity. Intolerance or allergy to certain foods may cause symptoms in your baby such as irritability, interrupted sleep, diarrhea, sneezing and wheezing, and tongue soreness. If your baby seems to react strangely to feedings, it's important to consult his doctor, who may recommend these steps:

- Note exactly what and when you feed your baby. Breast-feeding mothers should record their own food intake, as well.

- Discuss allergenic and hard-to-tolerate foods with your baby's doctor. Eliminate the most suspicious from your or your baby's diet for a week, and look for a change in his comfort level.

- When you have pinpointed your baby's sensitivity, test your hunch by reintroducing the culprit and noting whether the symptoms return.

- If your baby's symptoms are severe, consider having him tested for allergies.

With time and experimentation, you should be able to circumvent your baby's digestive difficulties and restore his post-feeding contentment.

Watch What You Eat
if You Breast-Feed

A diet heavy in onions or spicy foods can affect the taste of your breast milk. Consuming caffeine or gassy foods such as beans, raisins, or broccoli can lead to stomach discomfort in your baby.

Try for a Complete Breast-Feeding

Your baby's sucking need may be met before he is actually full. Music or another form of stimulation will help to keep him awake. Switch breasts earlier in the feeding, and talk to him, wipe his face, or change his diaper at the midpoint.

Monitor the Condition
of Bottle Nipples

Rubber nipples sometimes become clogged and can break down after being sterilized too many times. Latex nipples can tear. If your baby sucks or gulps more frantically than usual, it may be a sign that you need to make a change.

Consider Anti-Gas Drops

The inert ingredient simethicone can counteract your baby's digestive discomfort if you give it to him directly after a feed-

ing. Ensure that he gets a complete dose by squirting it directly into his mouth, rather than adding it to his bottle.

Offer Your Baby Warmed Bottles

Although cold formula quickly loses its chill as it passes to
the stomach, warm or room-temperature nourishment is often
more inviting to a baby.

Feed Your Baby on Demand

Some infants don't complain until their stomachs are completely empty; others like to feel full and start crying as soon as
they open their eyes. If your baby seems to need smaller, more
frequent feedings during the early weeks, it's a good idea to
comply.

Don't Wait Out Burps

Your hungry baby may protest vigorously if his feeding is
interrupted. It pays to remember that some infants don't burp
well and that others take in so little air, they require burping
only at the end of a feeding. Try burping your baby for thirty
seconds or so, then return him to the breast or bottle.

Look for Signs That
Your Baby's Needs Are Changing

During growth spurts, your little one may experience stronger
and more frequent hunger. To supplement his normal feedings,

offer him expressed milk, formula beyond the recommended thirty-two ounces, or cereal, whichever his doctor prefers.

Avoid Feeding
When a Comfort Object Will Do

If your bottle-fed baby suddenly begins waking at night, he may be looking for reassurance or company. Before offering him a bottle, try speaking to him softly, covering him with an extra blanket, or handing him a favorite doll.

It's not always easy to pinpoint the source of your baby's cries during feeding time. In fact, you may find yourself experimenting with—and discarding—any number of approaches before you understand exactly what your little one needs. By taking note of your baby's feeding habits, and by tailoring your responses to the patterns you observe, you'll soon eliminate the glitches. The system you develop is sure to replace frustration with warmth and closeness, making mealtime an event both you and your baby enjoy.

4

Crying Due to Physical Discomfort

Mark's three-month-old daughter seems to hate the outdoors. Though quite placid by nature, the baby wails in distress at each of her dad's attempts to expand her environment beyond the four walls of their home. "There's so much that I want the baby to see and hear," says Mark in frustration. "But our yard makes her so upset that I end up taking her back inside. I've even propped a bottle in her infant seat, hoping she'd forget where she was, but she ignores it. We may be destined to spend my daughter's formative years in the living room!"

Mark may not have considered the physical changes associated with a journey out of doors. The breeze that crosses his covered patio may chill his baby, who is accustomed to a near-constant room temperature. The daytime glare that has him fastening his daughter's sun hat may make the baby squint and squirm in misery. Babies, naturally, respond to their surroundings, reacting most strongly to those signals that change their comfort level. If your baby becomes chilled, overheated, itchy, sore, or otherwise bothered by a physical sensation, she'll cry as surely as she does when she is hungry. Chapter 4 contains information to help you identify your baby's cries of discomfort, along with suggestions for restoring calm and order to your baby's changing world. It's clear that your baby will be most receptive to new experiences when she feels good. This chapter will help you learn what her cries say about her state of comfort.

A TEST

Which responses are correct?

1. When your infant's mood suddenly turns sour, you should:
   a. teach her to calm herself by letting her fuss for a few minutes.
   b. check her carefully for the cause of her sudden misery.

2. Your baby suddenly stiffens her body and begins to howl. You should:
   a. chalk it up to colic, and settle in for a long afternoon.
   b. assume that her physical distress requires immediate attention.

3. Your usually content baby starts crying whenever you set her down. You should:
   a. mention this new tendency at her next health-care check-up.
   b. check her gums, skin temperature, and diaper area for a physical cause.

You have probably surmised that the correct response in each case is "b." As new parents quickly realize, a baby's crying isn't always related to hunger. When your little one's stomach can be ruled out as the source of her unhappiness, it's time to look for another cause.

WHAT YOU SHOULD KNOW

Babies experience the state of physical comfort just as adults do. However, their immature nervous systems and general sensitivity can make them react to environmental changes that adults don't notice, much less feel bothered by. Naturally, your little one lacks control over her environment. And when she encounters physical unpleasantness, she is unable to tell you what is wrong.

Your baby's gums may be inflamed due to teething. She may be feeling a poke or scratch from torn vinyl on her seat or play mat, or from a rough tag inside her clothing. Her delicate skin may be itchy or dry, or she may have a diaper rash that is making her miserable. She may be bothered by sudden darkness or bright light, or she may dislike the feel of suddenly humid air or the wind against her face. Her misery may be related to a problem with her bowels, or she may simply feel overheated or chilly.

Whatever the cause of your baby's discomfort, she wants relief from her distress just as an adult would. As you learn to read your baby's signals of unhappiness, you'll soon discover ways to make her more comfortable.

WHAT YOU'LL EXPERIENCE

Pinpointing the source of your baby's physical discomfort can be a challenge, but there are certain signs beyond her crying that can give you some direction. For instance, there's a good chance that teething is the culprit if she has begun gnawing or drooling a great deal, and her stools are looser than usual. An inflammation on her face, inside the folds of her skin, or in her diaper area can offer a clue to the cause of her misery, as will the appearance of a new scratch, abrasion, or pinpoint of blood somewhere on her body.

If your baby's discomfort is due to a change in her physical environment, she may squeeze her eyes shut as she cries, and turn her head or upper body to one side as if trying to get away. Or, she may screech and react with a jolt or stiffening of her body upon feeling a sting, chill, or similarly unpleasant sensation. A mottled, purplish look to areas of your baby's skin signal that she is crying because she feels cold, just as wet hair and dampness inside her body folds is evidence that she is unhappy about being hot.

If your baby's discomfort has no physical manifestation, the timing, pitch, and duration of her crying can still tell you a lot about the nature of her problem. By looking for a pattern or identifying a particular sensitivity, you'll be better able to make—and keep—your baby happy.

WHAT YOU CAN DO

The insets in this chapter offer valuable tips for coping with such infant maladies as diaper rash, skin inflammation, and bowel discomfort. What follows are additional suggestions regarding your baby's physical state.

Keep Lightweight Blankets on Hand

At home or away from home, a fleece or cotton receiving blanket is handy as a cover when out of doors or near a window. You can also use a blanket to block sunlight coming through a car window.

Check the Condition of Baby Gear

Vinyl mats and pads, infant seats, and swings deteriorate over time. Be alert to slits, rips, cracks, and holes in the nursery furnishings you use, particularly if any of them are hand-me-downs.

42

Skin Woes

As perfect as your baby's skin may seem, it is subject to a number of uncomfortable irritations. Here are suggestions for treating some common skin conditions:

- *Prickly heat.* This mild rash is composed of clusters of stinging red dots, and is caused by friction or excessive sweating. Avoid overdressing your baby, and use fabric softener when washing her clothes. When possible, machine-dry her clothes and linens.

- *Eczema.* Facial and body-fold sensitivity to dryness, chapping, or allergens can cause the skin to become rough and irritated. Use extra-strength, unscented moisturizing lotion, and talk to your baby's doctor about hydrocortisone cream.

- *Sunburn.* Babies' inadequate skin pigmentation causes them to burn easily. Consult a doctor if your baby's sunburn blisters or peels. For mild cases, dress her lightly, and apply cool cloths to the affected areas.

- *Impetigo.* This itching, burning infection occurs most often around the nose and mouth. Trim your baby's nails to prevent her from scratching the scabs, and consult her doctor about antiseptic or antibiotic treatment.

- *Nail problems.* Although a baby's nails are small and soft, they can trap dirt and germs, and leave angry scratches. Trim your baby's nails carefully—when she is asleep, if necessary—and often. Treat stinging scratches with an antiseptic.

- *Nickel allergy.* Nickel is a component of the metal in many snaps, buckles, and zippers. If your baby is sensitive to nickel, you'll notice small, rash-like marks wherever metal fastenings make skin contact. Look for plastic snaps and zippers in the clothing you buy, and coat the backs of the metal fastenings already in the baby's wardrobe with clear nail polish.

By treating your baby's skin problems promptly and by seeking medical advice when a condition seems to be worsening, you'll help keep your little one as comfortable as possible.

Examine Your Baby From Head to Toe

Look for cuts, scratches, and other sources of physical pain. Run your hand inside your baby's clothing, and check her diaper and the surface on which she is lying for sharp edges.

Avoid Environmental Extremes Whenever Possible

Do your errands and go on outings during the most temperate times of day. Try to ease your baby's transition from darkness to bright light, and vice versa.

Scrutinize Clothing Purchases

Remember that your baby's comfort is paramount. When shopping, look for soft garments that allow free movement,

---

Getting the Red Out

Even the most carefully tended baby bottom is subject to stinging and redness in the diaper area. Here's how to manage uncomfortable rashes:

- *Change your baby's diaper more often.* A raw bottom will heal faster if it's kept dry.

- *Avoid irritating substances.* Clean reddened areas with water only. Rinse diapers and baby clothes well.

- *Switch diapers.* Another type, material, or design may be better suited to your baby.

- *Diaper differently.* Maximize airflow by fastening the diaper loosely. Fold the gathers or liners away from the baby's skin.

- *Air-dry the skin.* Keep your baby's bottom bare during some of her wakeful periods.

- *Consider diet.* Antibiotics, teething, or changes in a breast-feeding mother's diet can affect the makeup of the baby's urine and stools.

   If all else fails, consult your baby's doctor. He or she is the best person to identify and treat serious diaper rashes.

---

and bypass the ones with features that might bind, poke, or rub against your baby's skin.

Remove Your Baby From an Environment That Makes Her Miserable

Be flexible enough to change your plans if your baby becomes uncomfortable. Often, moving away from an irritating stimulus saves you the trouble of identifying the exact cause of your little one's discomfort.

Be Alert to Bowel Sensitivity

Keep a log of the frequency and condition of your baby's uncomfortable bowel movements over several days. Then, discuss your and your baby's diet with your baby's doctor.

Protect Your Baby's Skin

Tuck a cloth diaper under your baby's chin when she feeds, and wipe any moisture from between the folds of her neck when she is finished. Bathe her only as needed, and rinse all soap carefully from her skin, hair, and the creases behind her ears.

Put a Barrier Between Your Baby's Skin and Drool

When your baby experiences episodes of increased drooling, use small, vinyl-backed bibs to keep the moisture away from her skin.

Address Teething Discomfort

To help your baby's teething progress, give her a frozen teething ring, or a hard biscuit or bagel. (Naturally, you will need to remain on hand to monitor her gnawing.) During

Issues of Elimination

Although bowel-movement patterns vary widely from baby to baby—and from day to day in a single baby—certain elimination symptoms can signal a potential problem. Here are some bowel problems to look out for:

- The absence of bowel movements for several days.

- The presence of blood in the stool.

- Watery stools or diarrhea.

- Stools that look black and tar-like.

- A stool that is yellow-brown and eliminated as a solid piece.

Only your doctor can determine whether your baby's bowel discomfort is due to constipation, diet, illness, or a more significant problem. Don't hesitate to consult with a professional if elimination difficulties arise.

painful episodes, consider asking your baby's doctor about the use of infant acetaminophen.

Give Your Baby a Back Rub

Your baby may feel better after a soothing massage, given to her while she lies facedown, clad in just a diaper, on your chest.

Summon Your Emotional Reserves

Pinpointing the cause of your baby's discomfort is important, but it's also important to remember that certain problems take a day or two to run their course. Be proud of yourself for having read your baby's signals, and be patient while the condition reverses itself.

Chalk It Up to a Bad Day

If you have ruled out all possible causes and your baby is still fretful, be willing to hold her more than usual and comfort her for the duration of her misery.

Your baby's daily requirements are as numerous as they are varied, and her needs become more complicated as her world expands. New sights and sensations may take your baby time to get used to. Or, a sensation may signal a problem, or remain so annoying as to be intolerable for months. Uncovering the source of the discomfort that is causing your baby to cry may take time and a bit of detective work. However, it's reassuring to know that a solution awaits you.

5

Crying Due to Medical Situations

Ten-month-old Jake, buckled into his stroller, was happily watching his father plant some flowers in the backyard when he suddenly went rigid and began to shriek. Stripping off his gardening gloves, Jake's father pulled the boy from the stroller, and hastily checked his face and body for a scratch, sting, or other cause for his obvious pain. He found nothing. As he put the screaming baby to his shoulder to rock him, he noticed the child pulling up his left shoulder and tilting his head downward on the same side. After another check of Jake's head and neck turned up nothing, the frantic father ran with the now inconsolable baby to a neighbor's house. Thinking quickly, the neighbor drove the pair to the emergency room, where, fifteen minutes later, a small beetle was pulled from deep inside Jake's ear.

Illnesses, accidents, and freak occurrences such as Jake's mishap are facts of childhood. When trouble arises, your baby certainly can't tell you what hurts, but the nature of his crying can reveal a lot. Chapter 5 offers guidelines on what to look for and how to respond when your baby's discomfort stems from routine sickness or something more serious. In medical situations, babies are dependent on adult knowledge and instinct. This chapter provides information that will help.

A TEST

Which of these statements are correct?

1. The presence or absence of fever isn't always an indicator of how a baby feels.

2. A baby's behavior and emotional needs can change during even a minor illness.

3. A baby will respond to efforts to soothe him even while enduring painful symptoms.

Actually, all of the above statements are true. Whether your baby is feeling mildly achy or in real pain, he is likely to cry more and in a different way than normal. When this happens, it pays to step up your usual TLC and exercise some special calming techniques.

WHAT YOU SHOULD KNOW

Having complete responsibility for a baby's health is frightening to many new parents. Your baby's first illnesses are sharp reminders of your lack of training. However, it should help you to know that you are not alone in your inexperience. Even medical professionals report feeling frantic and helpless when they become parents for the first time. More to the point, it is comforting to know that your confidence in your ability to handle medical situations will grow quickly.

It pays to be aware that your baby's doctor should address your insecurities just as he or she does your baby's medical condition. The right professional is at once approachable, supportive, and respectful of even trivial concerns. You may wish to "shop around" to find a doctor with whom you feel comfortable communicating.

At times, parents worry that giving extra TLC when suspecting an illness, but finding later that the baby's cries had no physical basis, may lead to spoiling the child. It's important to remember that babies aren't capable of manipulative behavior. Whether due to the pain of a sore throat or simple hunger, your baby's crying is his only method of conveying distress and the need for comfort. However you respond, your attentiveness will help him feel secure.

WHAT YOU'LL EXPERIENCE

You can sometimes tell when your baby's cries signal a medical condition rather than a wet diaper or other routine discomfort. His cry will often change from its ordinary fussy tone to a more pitiful, complaining, or, in some cases, frantic sound. The difference may be subtle or marked, depending on the circumstance—and the baby—but you'll soon develop a sixth sense about his different cries and what they mean.

Your suspicions about illness may be aroused by a change in your baby's demeanor. When he is noticeably less sociable or active than usual, if he avoids swallowing even at feedings, or if he moves in a way that draws your attention to his ear, abdomen, or bottom, it's a good indicator of where the problem lies.

You may find that your relationship with your sick baby also changes. Eating, sleeping, and other routines will be upset as your little one reacts to his discomfort. Communicating distress becomes his temporary focus, overshadowing any interest in eye contact, songs, or games that ordinarily earn a smile. Interaction may stop altogether if your baby's discomfort is particularly intense. For now, the techniques that usually work to calm his cries may be ineffective.

WHAT YOU CAN DO

Happily, there are steps you can take to try to lessen your baby's distress when he is in pain. Following are some helpful suggestions.

Stay in Touch With the Doctor

Find out if your baby's doctor has telephone hours or a nursing station available for parents who simply need information. Don't hesitate for a moment to call when you have a question.

Lessen the Pain of a Splinter or Insect Sting

If your baby has a splinter or was stung by an insect, cool the injured area with a cloth-wrapped ice cube. Then, using tweezers or your fingernails, pull the offending object out of your baby's skin.

Rule Out Emergencies

You'll feel calmer and more in control of the situation if you know that your sick baby is not in danger.

Make Your Baby Comfortable

Adjust the room temperature according to your sick baby's needs, and dress him in simple, fuss-free garments. Take steps to reduce his fever, if he has one.

Fighting Fever

A fever is a signal that your baby's immune system is hard at work against an infection or other medical condition. However, a baby's body temperature isn't well regulated, so temperatures between 97°F and 100°F don't necessarily signal sickness. A flushed face or a hot feel to the skin is often the best clue that a baby is coming down with an illness. Here are some steps to take when you notice these signs in your baby:

- Take your baby's temperature. Rectal and axillary (underarm) readings are still the most accurate. Avoid using ear and forehead thermometers.

- Call your baby's doctor if his temperature is over 101°F or under 97°F. Be prepared to report your baby's age, temperature, and unusual symptoms.

- For a high fever, dress your baby lightly and encourage him to feed often.

- For a low temperature, dress your baby warmly and seek immediate medical attention.

- If your baby's fever goes above 104°F, follow your doctor's advice about sponge baths and the use of acetaminophen. (Do not give your baby aspirin, which has been linked to Reye's syndrome. In addition, avoid bathing your baby with alcohol, which can be absorbed through the skin.)

High fevers can usually be brought down within a short period of time. By being alert to the signs of fever and by reporting troubling symptoms to the doctor, you'll best be able to keep your baby comfortable during bouts of illness.

The Lowdown on Ear Pain

Whether caused by a foreign object or an infection, ear pain can make anyone miserable. Here are some signs that your baby's uncharacteristic crying may be more than just irritability:

- Without warning, your baby stiffens, begins to scream, and cannot be consoled.

- Your baby pulls his head down to one side, or tugs or scratches at one ear.

- Your baby shows little or no interest in feeding.

- Your baby's breath has an unusual odor.

- Your baby is running a fever.

- You notice a discharge from one of your baby's ears.

Though some infections are unavoidable, you can lessen the potential for ear problems by keeping your baby away from people with colds, using only a washcloth to clean his ears, holding him at a 45-degree angle during feedings, and being attentive when he is handling finger foods or there are insects about.

Remain Calm

Your baby may be further upset by your tension. As long as the situation isn't a medical emergency, keep your movements sure and steady, and your voice soft and low as you tend to him.

Read Up on the Subject of Baby Health

When your baby is under the weather, it helps to be well versed in what to look for and what to do. Keep a baby-care guidebook or two on hand at all times.

Resist the Urge to Bundle Up Your Baby

Despite the potential for comfort, piling on blankets or hugging your baby close to you for extended periods impairs his ability to shed heat from his feverish skin.

Keep Your Baby Where He Can See You

Your sick baby may need extra reassurance, so move his infant seat or play mat from room to room as you tend to your chores and personal business.

Distract Your Baby From His Symptoms

Offer your baby something new to look at—a children's television show, perhaps—or play soft music on your stereo. You can also try gently massaging his back or limbs.

Consider the Potential for Motion Sickness

If car travel makes your baby miserable, he may be suffering from a queasy stomach. Try planning drives for times when the traffic is light or your baby is due for a nap.

Know the Usefulness of Cool Water

Running tap water helps to flush scrapes, minimize swelling, and reduce the pain of insect bites, bee stings, and minor sunburn.

Reduce Your Baby's Congestion

If your baby is upset because he cannot breathe through his nose, ask his doctor about using a nasal syringe or saline drops.

Stay Nearby

You'll be instantly alert to changes in your baby's condition and comfort level if you sleep in or just outside his room. Also, station someone at his side during the day.

Parents can't help but worry when their little one feels sick or in pain, but medical situations are bound to crop up during babyhood. As you become familiar with the different types of crying your baby does when he is hurting, you'll be quicker at

Red Flags

All babies get sick at one time or another, and their physical condition and behavior are often excellent clues to the nature of the illness at hand. Occasionally, though, symptoms can signal a potentially serious condition. Don't hesitate to contact your baby's doctor if you notice any of the following signs:

- Sudden, uncharacteristic shrieking that cannot be quieted.

- Sudden cessation of crying followed by a graying of the skin, lips, and nails.

- Crying that escalates sharply when you try to pick your baby up.

- Inconsolable crying after a fall.

- Moaning or whimpering that accompanies unusual lethargy, loss of movement in a limb, or a very high fever.

- Crying that is accompanied by labored breathing or swelling of the tongue, eyelid, or area surrounding an insect bite.

- Crying accompanied by blood in the stool, or a sudden protrusion in or swelling of the abdomen.

No one likes to imagine their baby in trouble, but emergencies do happen. You'll be best prepared to help your child if you're aware of the signs indicating that immediate medical attention is needed.

spotting trouble and more adept at minimizing misery. And, with increasingly less guesswork in the picture, both you and your baby will be happier.

6

Crying Out of Anger or Frustration

From the very start of her life, six-month-old Tara hated being bathed. At first, her parents thought that she felt chilly when undressed, but raising the room and water temperatures didn't make her cry any less. Experimenting with different water depths, moving her bath time to different hours of the day, and switching to tabletop sponge baths didn't help either. Tara still howled in fury. Desperate, the baby's parents purchased their third baby tub, a large model complete with an angled back, non-slip bottom, and toy holder. After filling the tub to a comfortable level, they lowered Tara into the water. She became hysterical before she was even fully wet. For now, Tara's parents have given up. Rather than begin each day with their daughter in a crying frenzy, they soap and rinse her during their own showers. The baby still dislikes the activity, but it is accomplished in fifteen seconds.

Even very young babies experience feelings of anger. When sufficiently frustrated, they express their agitation the only way they can—by crying. Chapter 6 discusses the kinds of things that trigger a baby's anger response and offers clues for knowing when frustration is the cause. It also presents suggestions for soothing the wails and tears that stem from annoyance. Although the experience of anger is a normal part of life, knowing how to handle your baby's angry crying will make it less upsetting for you both.

DO YOU RECOGNIZE THIS CHILD?

"My two-month-old flies into a rage when I interrupt her bottle-feeding, but it's important that I burp her."

"I hear a deep breath and an immediate howl of fury if I walk even twenty feet away from my eight-month-old."

"When my four-month-old realizes that I'm carrying her toward her play yard, she bursts into an angry wail."

Each of these parents was surprised to learn that babies can feel anger. They were further surprised to discover that everyday responses such as back-patting and rocking often do not work to soothe the crying that results from a baby's ire. Fortunately, there are approaches that have the desired calming effect.

WHAT YOU SHOULD KNOW

It may seem at first that babies, who command the limelight wherever they go and whose every need is met, would never have cause to become angry. But the fact is that babies do experience their own kinds of frustration, and these feelings can easily compel them to cry. Infants, for example, howl angrily at the sense of invasion that comes from being handled or fussed over by strangers, or poked and prodded by the doctor. The same outrage may be expressed at the removal of their current object of attention, be it a bottle, pacifier, or toy.

Older babies are similarly angered by restrictions imposed by the adults in their lives. Seatbelts, play yards, safety gates, and closed doors all keep little ones from exploring what and where they like, and are frequently met with wails of protest. Angry cries also often follow refusals to be allowed to climb on or handle items that are enticing, but pose a safety threat.

Babies are also frustrated by their growing awareness of their powerlessness. As they become more attuned to their surroundings, they discover the joy of learning by doing. They want to follow Mom and Dad everywhere, but can't move fast enough to do so. Physical limitations also get in the way of their ability to scale obstacles, perform fine motor tasks with any accuracy, and retrieve playthings that are out of reach. Inevitably, dozens of times each day, angry crying is the result.

WHAT YOU'LL EXPERIENCE

You may find that timing plays a part in triggering your baby's anger. Games and interactions that she normally finds entertaining will make her cry when she feels stressed. Your efforts to help with an activity that has her frustrated will usually have the same result.

Timing also plays a part in your baby's tolerance for adversity. There will be moments when your little one seems quite receptive to challenge and change. At other times, particularly when she is tired or overstimulated, she will seem to become frustrated by every activity.

You may also observe that your baby resists being patted, rocked, or even cuddled when she is angry. Intent on venting her frustration, your little one may be further irritated by your touch, however well intentioned. She may even react poorly to attempts to distract her from the obstacle at hand, particularly if the offered alternative is very familiar or if numerous items are presented in quick succession as a means of finding one that will catch her eye.

WHAT YOU CAN DO

The experience of frustration teaches resilience, but amid the confusion of everyday life, your baby may not always be receptive to this lesson. If the timing or duration of your little one's angry cries is a problem, you and she need not be at their mercy. Here are some calming tactics to try.

Verbalize Your
Baby's Frustration

Naturally, your child lacks the language to vent her feelings. Hearing your understanding tone may bring her up short and help her decompress.

Use Plastic Links
on Playthings

Stop tears over toys that fall out of reach by linking them to the side of your baby's high chair or play yard. Tossed playthings will dangle interestingly rather than skid across the floor. Eventually, your baby will be able to pull them back.

See That Your
Baby Stays Comfortable

Infants, in particular, react with outrage to stimuli that seem unpleasant. Guard against the sudden onset of chilly breezes, bright sunlight, and excessive heat.

Reading the Signs

Crying is the culmination of a baby's frustration. Often, negative feelings have been building for many minutes before the wails begin. Here are some common signs that your baby's anger is on the upswing:

- She shows prolonged awareness of an object pushed or tossed out of reach.

- Her body movements become tense and agitated.

- She makes tentative advances toward an object, followed by hasty retreats.

- Her facial muscles become tense, and you may see a frown.

- She jerks her body away from the source of her annoyance.

- Her grunts or whimpers become louder and more strident.

At first, it takes conscious effort to note clues that your baby is becoming angry enough to cry. Soon, however, reading your little one's body language will be second nature.

Be an Actor

Do your best to suppress your annoyance over your baby's frequent wails of frustration. Instead, distract your baby from her complaints with silliness or over-enthusiasm for whatever is next on your agenda.

Offer Calm,
Hands-On Help

Guide your baby physically through difficult or frustrating activities. Avoid the temptation to whisk away the source of her anger or to do the job for her.

Stay in Sight

Especially during clingy stages, your baby's angry cries may dwindle when you or her caregiver come into view. When you leave the room, speak to her from your new location to allow her to continue sensing that you are at hand.

Take Your Time

Hurrying a tense, frustrated baby will increase her agitation as surely as keeping a slow, steady pace will soothe her. Build enough extra time into your daily schedule to make rushing unnecessary.

Don't Take Your Baby's
Cries of Anger Personally

Remind yourself that a baby's primary caregiver is the natural target for most of her frustrated feelings, particularly during the second half of the first year. Have patience.

Choose Toys Carefully

Age recommendations are crucial not only as safety guidelines, but to ensure developmental appropriateness. Playthings geared toward your baby's age are less likely to frustrate her.

The Road to Rage

Because the transition from a state of curiosity to one of hysteria happens quickly in a baby, it is often difficult for parents to follow. In reality, the process usually has five steps:

1. *A sudden focus.* Your baby wants to attempt or explore something new. Or, she wishes to continue a pleasurable activity.

2. *A sense of helplessness.* Your baby discovers that she cannot do as she wishes, either because she lacks the physical ability or because an adult has intervened.

3. *Persistence.* Your baby's desire to continue her activity clashes with the force that is thwarting her efforts.

4. *Frustration.* Your baby is surprised and confused by her rising tension.

5. *Angry crying.* Your baby releases her tension outwardly through howls of outrage.

Seeing the steps that lead from curiosity to hysteria makes the quick transition more logical.

Have Distractions on Hand

Even when a baby is angry, nothing grabs her attention like the appearance of an unfamiliar plaything. Keep a few oddities hidden away in key rooms around your house.

Tear Stoppers

When it's time to nip your older baby's angry tears in the bud, it helps to have activities on hand that will pull her attention away from the source of her agitation. Here are several captivating ideas:

- Place a handful of Cheerios in a plastic-dispenser–type container.

- Pour a quarter-inch of dry oatmeal in the bottom of a flat pan.

- Drop an ice cube on your baby's high-chair tray. (Replace it when she is able to pick it up.)

- Give your baby an old magazine.

- Offer your baby a manipulative kitchen gadget, such as plastic measuring spoons or scissors-style tongs.

- Half-fill a small, capped, plastic soda bottle with water and food coloring.

Naturally, you will want to stay nearby as your baby explores these unfamiliar items or others of your own design. With luck, you'll find that their novelty banishes your baby's anger altogether.

Announce Your Approach

Calling out or singing as you move toward your agitated baby may distract her enough that her cries begin to wind down before you even reach her side.

Change Your Baby's Surroundings

If your baby's angry cries are gaining momentum, it may help to physically remove her from the object of her frustration. Hold her, even if she resists, and speak soothingly about an altogether different topic.

Don't Take Chances With Safety

If your baby's frustrated tears stem from limits you impose, resist the temptation to bend the rules so that she will calm down. Consistency can sometimes be difficult, but is most effective in the long run.

If you examine each episode of anger from your baby's perspective, it won't be hard to determine why she is upset. It will also be easier to think of a way to restore her contentment. With practice and patience, as well as sensitivity to your baby's changing moods, you can help life in your household run smoother.

7

Stress-Related Crying

Newborn Alex seems terrified by staircases. Unfailingly, he tenses and cries when going up a flight of stairs in his mother's arms. Descending is even worse. He flails his limbs and goes rigid, giving a horrified screech through clenched jaws. Then, he begins to wail in earnest. Alex's mother tries to grip the baby tightly to her body when using the stairs. She also moves very slowly and deliberately. However, neither tactic stops Alex's fearful crying. For the time being, the boy's parents have moved his bassinet, bathtub, and diapering station to the first floor of their home.

Alex is far from alone in his terrified response to something in his environment. Crowds and sudden or excessive noise reduce many babies to anxious crying. Other babies find the transition between activities, the sight of a strange face, or the absence of their primary caregiver to be unbearably stressful and cry inconsolably as a result. Chapter 7 discusses these and other anxiety producers, and provides hints for minimizing your baby's fearfulness, as well as his cries of stress. You cannot hope to eliminate all of the tension in your baby's life, but you can do certain things that may make his surroundings and activities more peaceful and enjoyable.

A TEST

Which of these statements applies to your baby?

1. My baby wails at the sight of his car seat.

2. My baby clings to me when he sees his grandmother.

3. My baby fusses when I rush around with him.

4. My baby shrieks at the sound of the vacuum.

5. My baby cries when I talk on the phone.

Babies are sensitive to various conditions in their environment, reacting with tension and insecurity to sights or events that make them feel uneasy. Whether your baby is made anxious by motion that he finds uncomfortable, a feeling of being ignored, or the sense that you are tense, he will often communicate his stress by crying. Though dealing with your baby's anxieties can be a matter of trial and error, there are things you can do to help him through sensitive stages.

WHAT YOU SHOULD KNOW

Given the commotion that characterizes everyday life, it is not surprising that infants become frightened by aspects of their surroundings—even in the face of the gentlest handling. Later, when they are better able to tolerate the presence of noise, crowds, and other strong stimuli, they still cry out of stress or fear about certain things. Such upset may be difficult for you to understand, particularly when the source of your baby's fright seems to change weekly, but the tension is very real to your baby. It pays to realize that your little one isn't likely to "get over" his fears through repeated exposure. Rather, he needs time away from the source of his unhappiness so that his anxiety, and his tears, can diminish.

For the most part, your baby needs to become familiar with new people, places, and activities before he can enjoy them. Too young to have expectations about a new experience, your baby may find the activity alarming and will tell you so by crying. Support and reassurance from you or his caregiver can help him better accept the unexpected.

If your baby is terrified of strangers, you should consider that it might be the actions of those strangers, rather than their appearance, that cause his crying. Wailing is the only way your baby can stop the unpleasantness when someone gets too close, is overly jolly, or handles him in a way that he finds irritating. Crying also tells of your baby's terror when you seem to have disappeared. As the hub of your little one's daily life, your absence, be it for a moment or a day, feels quite threatening. Ultimately, your baby's crying in fear is a call for you to take action.

WHAT YOU'LL EXPERIENCE

Your baby's behavior in circumstances he deems unpleasant can vary widely. If he is frightened by excess motion or handling, or hates confinement and restraint, he may punctuate his screams by stiffening his body as he physically repels your efforts to bathe, dress, move, or cuddle him. He may also squeeze his eyelids shut and toss his head, refusing eye contact as if doing so could cause you and your demands of him to disappear. A less physical baby may press himself against you as if willing himself to be shielded from the source of his fright or spirited to a less stressful place.

A baby whose anxiety is a response to the people in his surroundings will seem suspiciously watchful, signaling his rising tension by a whimpering that quickly escalates to full-scale crying. If he is mobile, he may scramble desperately after you, wailing to be picked up and then refusing to be set down even after he has stopped crying. As if to make a certain stranger disappear, he may even bury his face against your shoulder.

If your baby is frightened by a particular stimulus, be it the feel of your carpet, the sight of your neighbor's dog, or the sound of the dishwasher, he will startle and howl at each recurrence. He may cling to you or go completely rigid as he cries, and be unable to relax until removed from the scene. Whatever the source of your baby's stressful cries, your care and sensitivity to what frightens him will encourage him to become more tolerant of his environment.

WHAT YOU CAN DO

How can you help your anxious baby feel less stressed by his day-to-day experiences? In general, it is helpful to adopt a slow, gentle, reassuring pace that has building your baby's sense of security as a primary goal. The following ideas can help you in this endeavor.

Respond Consistently to Your Baby's Cries

Your baby's sense of security will grow as he learns that he can count on your help when he communicates fright or stress. Even if his anxiety seems frequent and excessive, offer him comfort when he cries.

Separate Your Baby From the Source of His Fear

Don't assume that repeated exposure will help your baby feel more comfortable with what frightens him. He'll be calmer if you let his tension level dictate what—and who—surrounds him.

Creating Calm

Sights, sounds, and motion can be fascinating to a baby. But sometimes, distraction is exactly what your infant doesn't need. Here are several potential trouble spots:

- *Crowds.* The line between exciting and overwhelming is a fine one. The bustle and commotion that accompany large groups of people is too much for many babies to bear.

- *Noise.* Infants have minimal ability to filter out sounds. Loud, sudden, or blended noise can be unpleasant to many babies.

- *Napping on the run.* Some babies can sleep almost anywhere. However, interrupted sleep isn't always restful and can play havoc with your baby's ability to cope with stress.

- *Lights and colors.* Babies have different thresholds for visual stimulation. A constant array of sights can be overwhelming or so captivating that a baby cannot relax.

- *Siblings and friends.* The sight of children at play is very entertaining. However, their laughter, noise, and quick movements can be stressful to a tired or overstimulated baby.

- *Too much touch.* Sensations and motion may delight or endlessly annoy your baby. But, even infants who thrill to tactile stimulation can feel bombarded by too much petting or rocking.

How much stimulation is too much? The answer differs with each baby. As you learn to read your infant's moods, you'll soon know when and how to quiet things down.

Stay Connected

Step up the amount of time you spend playing with your baby. Make frequent eye contact, show him things, and play games. When your baby tires of you, move away, but continue to chat with him from afar. He is likely to stay calmer in your presence.

Minimize Bumping and Jostling

Motion and body movement may further upset some fearful babies. Try swaddling your little one in a receiving blanket, or holding him chest to chest while you lie flat.

Help Your Baby to Calm Himself

Place your baby on his back so that he can twist, curl up, or stretch as he chooses. If sucking soothes him, gently guide his fingers or fist toward his mouth.

Avoid the Urge to Cuddle

Many older babies use movement to calm themselves. Hugging your little one tightly deprives him of this chance to move away from the source of his tension.

Be Honest About Your Departures

Avoid sneaking away, which may cause your baby to feel insecure and fearful. Even if face-to-face good-byes cause him to cry, he will eventually come to trust in your return.

Have Distractions Readily Available

Your anxious baby may be soothed by the sight of a moving object—a ceiling fan or mobile, for instance. Or, he may quiet down upon hearing a familiar droning noise, tune, or song.

Adopt Certain Phrases

Using set statements, such as "I'll be right back" before momentary departures or "I'll see you at five" before leaving for work, will give your baby a comforting sense of familiarity.

Establish a Set Childcare Arrangement

Whatever your work schedule, set up a childcare plan on which your baby can count. A sense of routine will add to his sense of security.

Play Your Baby's Way

It's no secret that your baby's temperament can differ from yours. Therefore, it isn't always easy for you to think of activities that he will find pleasurable. The trick is to keep his likes and dislikes in mind when you plan. To help, ask yourself the following questions:

- Do excessive touch and motion upset your baby? For now . . .

  Do place him on a colorful mat at playtime.
  Don't buckle him in for a bike ride.

- Does your baby thrill to movement? For now . . .

  Do invest in a baby swing and stroller.
  Don't use his high chair for playtime.

- Is your baby an alert observer? For now . . .

  Do take him to a ballgame, a farm, or a pier.
  Don't rely on music for his entertainment.

- Do unusual sounds frighten your baby? For now . . .

  Do keep appliances off during his playtime.
  Don't set up his play yard out-of-doors.

Naturally, your baby's taste for different activities will change along with his acceptance of new things. By keeping his sensitivity in mind, you'll develop a knack for play that pleases him.

Create a Quieter Environment

Speak softly and move slowly when caring for or playing with your baby. A quiet, gentle pace may help your baby feel secure.

Is Your Baby Easily Stressed?

Anxious babies' frequent crying is their way of communicating fear and distress. They also tend to be:

- *Highly sensitive.* Your baby may be very much attuned to changes in his surroundings.

- *A light sleeper.* Your baby's naps may be brief, and he may awaken numerous times during the night.

- *Tense.* Your baby may seem unable to relax or to lie quietly.

- *Wiry.* Cuddling your baby may be difficult because he tends to stiffen.

- *Intense.* Your baby's moods may be fleeting, and reach extreme highs and lows.

- *Inconsistent.* There may be little pattern to your baby's needs and behavior.

It may help you to consider that your anxious baby's demands may develop into something positive. The emotional traits that make him difficult today may re-emerge as a strength and focus that will serve him well in life.

Allow for Warm-Up Time

When another adult enters the room or you return from an absence, allow your anxious baby time to feel comfortable. Stay at arm's length until he makes eye contact or otherwise indicates that he is ready to interact.

Rock Your Baby to Sleep

At night, you may be able to put down your anxious baby only if he is in a deep sleep. After feeding and changing him, try rocking him for fifteen minutes before placing him in bed.

Scale Down Your Baby's Activities

For now, keep errands and outings that involve your baby to a minimum. A quiet day is likely to bring less anxiety and upset than a busy one.

Though your baby's fearful stages may seem long and difficult to endure, your presence and your patience give him what he needs to grow more peaceful and secure. By adopting your baby's pace and by acting on the cues he sends about new experiences, you'll be able to anticipate his alarm, communicate reassurance, and help him be more accepting of things.

8

Crying for Attention

For the past two weeks, ten-month-old Jessica has developed a crying pattern that begins like clockwork at nine o'clock each morning. She awakens at around seven-thirty and has breakfast immediately, so her parents have ruled out fatigue or hunger as the source of her misery. And, though she calms down as soon as someone interacts with her, she can't seem to stay settled. Unable to accomplish much at home in the face of her baby's morning crankiness, Jessica's mother has begun to run her errands at this time of day. Out and about, Jessica is calm and happy.

Jessica's mother may have unwittingly hit upon the cause of her baby's morning crying. Jessica has two older siblings and has difficulty adjusting to the sudden quiet after they leave for school. Endlessly amused when watching her brothers at play, Jessica lacks practice at playing alone and may be crying from boredom. Morning outings provide the stimulation she craves. Some babies are good at entertaining themselves, while others become fussy when interaction is lacking. Chapter 8 discusses a baby's need for attention and presents tactics for calming cries that stem from boredom. This chapter also presents ideas for keeping your baby stimulated.

DO YOU RECOGNIZE THIS CHILD?

"My baby seems like she is easily bored."

"I'm afraid my child isn't very good at playing by herself."

"Should I pick my baby up every time she cries?"

Comments and questions like these are often uttered by parents whose babies seem to require a lot of attention. Alert, active, and demanding, these babies are happiest when face to face with someone. In a quiet environment, or in the absence of interaction, their restless displeasure quickly surfaces as crying.

WHAT YOU SHOULD KNOW

An attention-seeking baby is often a very sociable being—alert, watchful, and happiest amid the bustle of people and activity. Typically, she thrills to social games and chitchat, and quickly finds that her favorite pastime is watching other people. When the conversation stops or her entertainer leaves the room, the attention-seeking baby feels a sense of abandonment, which she lacks the tools to dispel. Bored and alone, she will communicate her sadness in a most effective way—by crying.

If your baby seems demanding, but not particularly social, she may be crying for attention simply to keep you at hand. The stages of dependence vary in their timing and duration, and your baby needs to feel secure and emotionally at ease before she can begin to enjoy solitude or venture forth to explore her surroundings. While some babies seem to detach quickly from their caregivers, many need extra time and additional reassurance to feel a sense of security. You need not worry that your baby's seeming over-attachment is a reflection of your parenting ability.

It helps to anticipate that your baby's dependence level will fluctuate. She may go through periods of enjoying solitary play, but then enter a phase during which she needs adult support in order to explore happily. Remember that your baby's crying isn't meant to be manipulative. She is merely communicating her need for companionship.

WHAT YOU'LL EXPERIENCE

If your baby is an attention-craver, you may feel as if your waking hours are spent at her beck and call. She may coo and smile as you care for and play with her, but seem suspiciously alert to your attempts to move away or even turn your eyes elsewhere. Sensing that she has lost your attention, she will begin to fuss and, most likely, regain it at once.

If your baby is particularly alert and curious, you may find that her demanding cries are linked to frustration or even overstimulation. In her desire to experience everything around her, your baby may attempt things that are beyond her ability. Or, she may overdo her exploration and cry to be removed from a situation that suddenly feels threatening.

You will probably find that no one technique works consistently to keep your baby content. Her taste in entertainment is likely to change as she grows. The novelty of playthings, games, and activities will wear off quickly. In addition, there will be days when she feels tired or otherwise out of sorts, and simply cannot summon the focus necessary to enjoy even her most beloved pastime. Crying for attention may signal restlessness or meltdown as often as it conveys boredom.

WHAT YOU CAN DO

A baby who is bored or restless is surely crying for attention. However, it is unrealistic to think that you can be constantly available to her. You may find that distracting her with a new stimulus is often a perfectly acceptable substitute for socializing. In this vein, following are some strategies to try.

Keep Up the Conversation

Questions and chatter in varied tones and volumes can keep your baby's attention for surprising lengths of time. Even from across the room or around a corner, your voice can satisfy your baby's need for socialization.

Periodically Change Your Baby's Surroundings

Stave off boredom by setting up play areas in several rooms of the house. Occasionally, pair your little one with a same-aged playmate. Investigate playgroups, gym classes, and library programs geared toward babies.

Vary What Your Baby Views

Be alert to your little one's fascination with lighting patterns, or the movement of curtains or a fan. Try to offer more of the same kind of stimulation. Also, pique her social side by showing her photos of other babies.

Develop Special Songs

When you find a rhyme, rhythm, or verse that seems to please your baby, make frequent use of it. Singing or chanting familiar words and phrases can have great entertainment power.

The Up Side of Attachment

Though your baby's cries for attention may seem excessive, her strong attachment to you has a number of distinct benefits.

The attention-getting baby feels freer to explore and so is quicker to learn about her surroundings. She learns empathy and sensitivity from your consistent, loving responses to her. She develops a sense of security that makes her more trusting and less afraid.

Very attentive parents have a strong sense of their baby's personality and emotionality. They develop a clearly defined, well-thought-out parenting style. They avoid unnecessary frustration by recognizing and heading off potential trouble.

The next time your baby's demands loom large, try to focus on the satisfying results you will see in the future.

Make Use of Music

Audiocassettes, children's television programs, and even radio stations featuring country, classical, or other music can provide ongoing entertainment. Repetition of familiar tunes may be particularly pleasing to your baby.

Use a Night-Light

Low lighting gives your baby something to gaze at as she drifts off to sleep at bedtime. Since recent research links long-term night-light use with later eye problems, you may wish to turn off the light once your baby is asleep.

Position Your Baby
So She Can Look Around

An infant seat or swing will allow your little one to sit upright during her wakeful periods. For a change of position and a chance to stretch, place her on her back on a blanket or quilt.

Allow Your Baby
Free Movement

Baby-proof the rooms in which your little one plays so she can roll, crawl, or toddle around safely and at will. Avoid leaving her for long periods in a play yard.

Watch for Signs of
Increased Tension

A baby who is becoming overstimulated often exhibits the same signs of discomfort and restlessness as one who is bored. Try moving your child to a calmer, quieter location.

Avoid Overtiring
Your Baby

A calm, rested baby is more open to environmental stimuli and better able to amuse herself. Don't expect your child to play well alone if naptime is approaching.

Are Fussing and Crying the Same Thing?

When your baby whimpers and complains, she is often getting ready to cry. However, parents who wait out those initial grunts and squirms often find that their fussy baby calms herself down. Sometimes, a change of scenery or adjustment in routine may be all that is needed to get your baby through a bad moment. Other times, she may distract herself and quiet down on her own.

Naturally, your baby's cries warrant your attention. However, if your baby's fussing only escalates to real crying when your face comes into view or you pick her up, it may be worthwhile to delay your response and give her the opportunity to settle down by herself.

Note the Timing of Your Baby's Demanding Periods

If your baby always cries when you prepare dinner or her older sibling goes out to play, try moving her about or adjusting your routine to keep her feeling like she's a part of things.

Rotate Your Baby's Playthings

Babies quickly tire of familiar items, no matter how engaging they are. Try separating your baby's toys into three bins and giving her access to just one group at a time. After a few weeks, make a change.

Can You Spoil Your Baby?

Two generations ago, parents were warned against spoiling their babies with too much attention. Then, studies showed that babies whose complaints were answered quickly developed sophisticated communication styles that replaced crying. This led to mixed feelings about letting babies "cry it out."

Today, the popular viewpoint lies somewhere in between. Any parents who have sat up all night with a sick baby or left their little one in the care of a fawning relative can attest to how quickly a settled baby can resume round-the-clock demands for your attention.

Can you spoil your baby? Many experts say that this occurs when parents try to spare their baby frustration, thereby letting her moods rule the entire household. Seizing upon quick solutions—4:00 A.M. car rides, say—to long-term problems such as sleeplessness denies your baby the chance to act for herself. It also keeps you at her beck and call.

Keep Your Baby's Toys in Order

Babies tend to pay little attention to playthings that are piled haphazardly. Taking the time to re-stack and reassemble toys after each playtime may make these items more inviting to your baby.

Understand the Power
of Your Attention

Keep a basket of oddities on hand to substitute for your attention, and to occupy your baby while you talk on the telephone or tend to a chore. Buy time by delaying eye contact with your baby until you are ready to pick her up.

Be Willing to Step In
If Your Baby Really Needs You

A massage, a walk out-of-doors, or some ordinary conversation may be the only thing that will restore your attention-seeking baby's good spirits. Be willing to alter your agenda on fussy days.

The type of attention your baby craves depends on her personality and social style. Whether she appears to like solitude, but tires quickly of her playthings, or seems completely miserable without adult attention, a change of pace may please her. With a bit of experimentation, you will soon learn which activities and interactions keep her most entertained and happy.

9

The Rest of the Family

Mary Judson's two-month-old baby had been crying all morning. In need of a few minutes' peace, the young mother placed her squalling infant in his bassinet. But, she hurried back to the nursery when the baby's cries took on a sudden panicked note. To Mary's horror, she found her three-year-old half-dragging, half-carrying the wailing infant toward an open closet. "I putting brother away," said Mary's firstborn in response to his mother's outrage. "He be quiet then."

As much a hallmark of infancy as crying may be, a baby's yowls of misery can wrack the nerves of your entire family. Chapter 9 explores the effect of frequent crying on parents and siblings, and offers strategies for coping with this most demanding aspect of a baby's first year. Infancy is characterized by unpredictability and uncertainty. This chapter provides information and advice that will help your family cope with this very stressful time.

DO YOU RECOGNIZE THIS FAMILY?

"Mama, I no like baby."

"My new sister has ruined everything!"

"Honey, can't you shut the baby up?"

Comments like these might take aback the average listener, but they'll hardly raise an eyebrow if heard by someone in a newly expanded household. Why? Because the effects of listening to hours of baby cries are dramatic, family-wide, and well documented. Whether you're age two or age forty-two, it's impossible to overstate the tension wrought by a colicky or cranky baby who resists every effort to calm him. Parents feel helpless, siblings feel angry, and the whole family feels guilty for resenting their tiny intruder. With its huge demands on your energy and patience, the newborn stage may seem a time to endure rather than to enjoy.

WHAT YOU SHOULD KNOW

New parenthood requires a tremendous amount of energy, largely because of the many uncertainties of life with an infant. Is your baby developing on schedule? Are you handling him safely? Are your responses consistent and correct? Are you meeting the needs of your other family members? There's a lot to consider—and to worry about—as your infant assumes his place in the family and you resolve to take one day at a time.

Suddenly, though, this fragile balance is upset. Where baby sniffles and sighs were the norm, longwinded squalls of misery take over. Almost overnight, your peaceful newborn becomes an angry stranger, and you become consumed with consoling him. Soon, you're so weary and frustrated that each baby wail seems larger than life. Your spouse balks at your testiness, which fuels resentment and self-pity. If you have other children, they're so unsettled by your remoteness and tension that they change their own behavior in an effort to restore normalcy to the household.

As frightening as the overall picture may be, these changes in family dynamics are perfectly normal. More important, they need be only temporary. By fostering the right attitude toward your baby's days or weeks of prolonged crying, you can see to it that your family emerges from the infant experience with a new respect for individual needs and a new resolve to handle problems as a unit.

WHAT YOU'LL EXPERIENCE

There's no question that the arrival of a fussy infant changes family life considerably. However, it's interesting to note that the effect of a baby's crying varies according to the listener's role. Following is a look at the aftermath of all the howling:

- *The individual.* Studies show that the sound of a baby's crying triggers a defensive physical response similar to that of a person under siege. You react involuntarily with an adrenaline rush that creates muscle tension, sweaty palms, and a rapid heartbeat. Instinctively, you may wish to flee, but in reality, you must do just the opposite—confront and win over the enemy. And you must do this despite your tired, emotionally fragile state.

- *The couple.* Your pre-baby partnership changes dramatically as you concentrate your energy on calming your demanding infant. For now, there's little interest in workday issues or the state of your marriage, as you and your partner each believe that you're shouldering as much responsibility as you can handle. You may connect with your spouse only while doing housework or baby-care chores, and wonder why you're not bothered by the absence of your former intimacy. Occasionally, you mourn the loss of relaxed conversation and a physical relationship. More often, though, you numbly accept living as teammates instead of lovers, and await the time you will regain enthusiasm for one another.

- *The parents.* Life with a fussy infant probably bears little resemblance to the cozy mental picture you formulated during pregnancy. If this is your first child, you most likely never imagined you would be living with constant interruptions and upset plans. You never considered how fatigue would undermine your vow to respond lovingly and consistently to your infant's needs. If this baby is your second, you're wondering what happened to your plans for tandem naps, side-by-side play, and general sibling harmony. You're trying to be flexible, but your baby's unpredictable crying causes you great stress. You feel isolated, your self-confidence has taken a nosedive, and, as your anxiety builds, your family's needs seem impossible to meet.

- *The siblings.* Older children react strongly to the arrival of a new brother or sister, and are quick to resent the accompanying noise, distraction, and change in routine. To a child, your baby's many demands are an inconvenience; your stress an unpleasant state for which the baby is solely to blame. Siblings grow anxious as tension builds during each episode of crying, for they feel pushed aside—often, rightfully so. They see little use for the newcomer who spoils their plans, takes up all your time, and appears to please no one in the family.

All in all, the effects of your baby's frequent crying can combine to form a rather depressing picture, however temporary. There's good news, though, in that you *can* make this stage easier for your family to endure.

WHAT YOU CAN DO

When it seems that your whole family is unraveling at the hands of its youngest member, it's better to take a positive stance than to dwell on how difficult your days and nights have become. Taking action, however small, can help restore your sense of control over the daily workings of your household. The strategies that follow can give you the sense that you are doing something about your baby's frequent crying and can help your family keep the noise and commotion in perspective.

Get Comfortable With Your Baby

Spend time holding and handling your infant to dispel the tentativeness that often characterizes the parent-newborn relationship. You'll find yourself feeling more protective, and your baby will draw comfort from your touch.

Put Your Fears to Rest

If you are worried that your baby's crying is due to a physical ailment or a problem with your parenting skills, discuss the matter with your baby's doctor. You'll gain peace of mind from the professional assurance that nothing is wrong.

Know Your Stress-Tolerance Level

Try not to put yourself in situations that create additional tension during an already difficult time. For now, delegate office projects, postpone large chores, call in childcare favors, and avoid entertaining.

Look on the Bright Side

Frequent crying isn't all bad, say child development experts. In fact, there are several distinct benefits to those seemingly endless whimpers and wails. The next time a difficult day threatens to fray your nerves, remember that your baby's crying:

- Serves as an emotional outlet for releasing tension.

- Encourages the development of speech by triggering awareness of the lips, tongue, palate, and vocal chords.

- Alerts you to problems, needs, and mood changes, thereby enabling you to relax whenever he is calm and quiet.

The most important benefit of your baby's crying lies in your response to his distress. Your consistent appearance to comfort and soothe him teaches your little one that he can count on your help whenever he needs it. This will help him feel secure and confident.

Eliminate Your Worst Stress Triggers

Identify the circumstances that make you extra tense—when your baby's nap is interrupted, say, or when he howls throughout dinner. Do what you can to change your routine so that you can concentrate on your baby's needs during those times.

Be Honest

Give yourself permission to feel frustrated, and don't hesitate to voice any angry or ambivalent feelings that may strike during your baby's fussy periods. Your coping difficulties may be cries for help, but they're not signs of weakness.

Listen and Observe

Look for a correlation between your baby's crying and your partner's emotional ups and downs. If you are not your baby's primary caregiver, voice your appreciation of the stress inherent in infant care and take the initiative to lighten the load of the other parent.

Put Yourself on Your To-Do List

Appreciate the fact that you need a certain amount of nurturing to function at full capacity. Get out by yourself twice a week—even for fifteen minutes—and look for ways to incorporate a personal interest into your new schedule.

Be a Couple

As short as you may be on energy, your relationship with your partner needs attention. Refocus on one another by getting out twice a month without your baby. Do something that refreshes you, be it exercising, visiting friends, or taking in a movie.

Are You in Sync With Your Baby?

"He's just like his dad!"

"He reminds me so much of my brother as a baby!"

Do these family comparisons sound familiar? When it comes to temperament, children usually take after a close relative, according to learning-styles specialist Lauren Bradway, PhD, coauthor of *How to Maximize Your Child's Learning Ability.* But that family member may not be you!

"An innate attraction to sights, sounds, or motion guides most aspects of your baby's development," says Dr. Bradway. "If you and your baby happen to have different sensory preferences, your likes and dislikes will also differ." Here's how to tune in to your baby's sensory style:

- *Decide whether visual, auditory, or tactile stimulation most pleases your baby.* Base your soothing techniques not on what *you* find calming, but on what captivates *him.*

- *Engage your baby's preferred sense when you interact with him.* If he is active, bounce your knee while feeding or cuddling him. If he is sociable, sing and talk a lot. If he's very alert, fill his environment with colors and patterns.

- *Avoid sensory overload.* Your little one at first will be unable to shut out the sights, sounds, or movements he finds so appealing. Depending on his sensory preference, help him get to sleep by darkening the room, drowning out noise with a fan, or swaddling him tightly.

When you view your baby's behavior as an offshoot of inborn sensory style, you'll be better able to understand him and keep him happy.

Be Specific
About the Help You Need

Make a list of the obligations you are having trouble meeting due to the demands of caring for your baby. Then, share the list with your family. Request assistance, and hand over responsibility for the most important items on the list.

Agree to Separate at Night

Determine which parent needs the better night's sleep, and have him or her bed down in the part of the house that is farthest from where the baby sleeps. Trade places on weekends to give the primary caregiver two restful nights in a row.

Hold Frequent Meetings
With Your Older Children

Talk with your older children about the baby's helplessness and the time he needs to settle into the family. Ask your children for baby-calming ideas and suggestions for improving the household routine.

`Market the Role of*
Big Brother/Big Sister

Older siblings will look more kindly on the baby if they are made to feel somewhat superior. Give them a few new privileges, tell them about their infant antics, and commiserate with them as teammates during the most difficult days.

Keep Older Children Occupied

Ask your spouse, relatives, and friends for help entertaining your older children—preferably, away from your house. Their excitement about these outings can help offset any new-baby resentment they feel. In addition, you'll feel less pressed to maintain good cheer.

Set Guilt Aside

Remind yourself that some 25 percent of newborns can be classified as high-need babies, with nearly 40 percent experiencing some degree of colic. Your infant's crankiness can't be blamed on you, your spouse, or the other children in your home.

Join a Parents' Group

No one understands what life with a fussy baby is like better than someone who is sharing the experience. Networking with other new parents will bring sympathy, support, fresh ideas, and reassurances that this difficult stage will pass.

Seek Advice

Talk to friends and relatives about their days as new parents, and ask them to recall specific baby-calming techniques that

Ideas
for Siblings

It isn't always easy to keep an older child happily occupied while tending to a baby. Here are a few keep-busy suggestions:

- *Water play.* Put two inches of water in the kitchen sink or bathtub, and give your child an assortment of spoons and plasticware, a footstool (if necessary), and a towel or two for mop-ups.

- *Pen pals.* Give your child some paper, stickers, and age-appropriate writing implements, and have him or her write to or draw a picture for an out-of-town relative or friend.

- *Mail call.* Give your child unwanted catalogs and interesting-looking junk mail to open and sort through as "his" mail. Save new items that arrive in a box or basket for when needed.

- *Kitchen projects.* Have your child spoon out slice-and-bake cookie dough, create an original snack mixture, or play with a tray of dry oatmeal.

- *Water painting.* Give your child a two-inch paintbrush and a small pail of water, and invite him to "paint" the front steps, deck, driveway, or wooden fence.

Planning a few special activities can keep your first-born happily occupied during his younger sibling's fussy periods—and help to restore peace to your home.

worked for them. The next time your baby seems inconsolable, you'll be able to respond with some new tactics.

Keep a Record of Your Baby's Fussy Periods

Though your baby's crying may seem constant, it may really fall well within the normal limits for an infant—up to two hours daily the first month, and up to four hours daily the second month.

Laugh

When you've done all that you can and your baby is still screaming, use humor to help your family cope. Try comparing your mood to the baby's, guessing what he'd say if he could talk, or debating which relative or television personality his reddened face calls to mind.

Couples who are used to well-ordered lives are sure to be uncomfortable relinquishing control to an eight-pound infant. But, the simple truth is that you cannot organize the life of a young baby. For a good part of your baby's infancy, a schedule will be anything that he does more than twice in a row.

Don't despair, for this unpredictability is but a stage. More important, don't abandon your efforts to help your little one settle down, no matter how fruitless those efforts sometimes seem. Research has shown that a parent's attempts to calm a baby have more effect than usually thought. Your baby may howl through your attempts to cradle, rock, and soothe him, but your closeness will make him feel less anxious and, often, less miserable. Leaving him to his own devices will almost certainly cause him to escalate his crying.

Parenting a fussy baby is a huge responsibility, but it isn't all stress and hard work. Over time, every whimper, shriek, and howl is sure to be offset by a moment that warms your heart. Make it a point to keep your baby's worst days in perspective and to carefully store memories of his good ones. The trials and the joys of his special first year will be over before you know it.

Conclusion

Kyle was a fussy infant who required a lot of adult attention to stay happy. Rocking did little to quiet his wails; but sometimes, he would calm to the sound of his mother's voice and sometimes to the sight of a certain toy or a neighborhood child at play. Why, his mother wondered, was there no set technique that could be counted on to soothe him? Why did soft music or a ride in the car work wonders to stop his crying on some occasions, but not on others?

That puzzled mom was me, more than ten years ago. And over time, as it became more clear that I needed different approaches to soothe my baby during his many and varied crying episodes, I made another profound discovery—the rocking that so often irritated my first baby nearly always quieted my secondborn, Brad. Yet, the same swaying motion could be counted on to send Emily, my third child, into hysterics. So, not only do parents need to pinpoint why their baby is crying and then use a trial-and-error approach to identify the source of the upset, they must also determine if their baby is more likely to respond to visual, auditory, or sensory stimulation—or, more accurately, if the calming method they are about to use might actually worsen the baby's fussy mood.

A tall order? Yes, particularly for the parents of the many babies whose dispositions during the early months are less than sunny. If you have chosen to read *Hush Little Baby*, your child is probably among the large number that seem to spend a lot of time in an unhappy state. This is perfectly normal, of course, but both you and your little one will feel better once you have developed the knack for restoring his contentment. No doubt you already know that the "one size fits all" rule doesn't work with babies. That is why I have supplied a collection of techniques from which you can choose on your baby's fussy days. May you be a more confident, more effective parent for having applied some of the tactics within these pages.

Suggested Reading List

For additional help with identifying and calming your baby's many cries, you may wish to browse through some of the following books. Most can be found at your local bookstore or ordered directly from the publisher. The older titles that are out of print are available at many public libraries.

Ayllon, Ted. *Stopping Baby's Colic.* New York: Perigee Books, 1989.

Green, Diana S. *79 Ways to Calm a Crying Baby.* New York: Pocket Books, 1988.

Hill, Barbara Albers. *Baby Tactics: Parenting Tips That Really Work.* Garden City Park, NY: Avery Publishing Group, 1991.

Jones, Sandy. *Crying Baby, Sleepless Nights.* Boston: Harvard Common Press, 1992.

Sammons, William A.H. *The Self-Calmed Baby: A Liberating New Approach to Parenting Your Infant.* Boston: Little, Brown & Co., 1989.

Sears, William. *Keys to Calming the Fussy Baby.* Hauppauge, NY: Barron's, 1991.

Sears, William. *Parenting the Fussy Baby and High-Need Child: Everything You Need to Know From Birth to Age 5.* Boston: Little, Brown & Co., 1996.

Shukat, Evelyn. *Why Is My Baby Crying? A Practical Guide to What Bothers Babies and Worries Parents During the First Six Months of Life.* New York: Villard Books, 1986.

Solter, Aletha J. *Tears and Tantrums: What to Do When Babies and Children Cry.* Goleta, CA: Shining Star Press, 1998.

Index